Recent Trends
in Social
Learning Theory

CONTRIBUTORS

JUSTIN ARONFREED

ALBERT BANDURA

J. ALLAN CHEYNE

BRIAN COATES

JACOB L. GEWIRTZ

WILLARD W. HARTUP

ROSS D. PARKE

RECENT TRENDS IN SOCIAL LEARNING THEORY

Edited by **ROSS D. PARKE**

*The Fels Research Institute for
the Study of Human Development
Yellow Springs, Ohio*

 1972

ACADEMIC PRESS   New York and London

ACADEMIC PRESS, INC.
111 Fifth Avenue, New York, New York 10003

United Kingdom Edition published by
ACADEMIC PRESS, INC. (LONDON) LTD.
24/28 Oval Road, London NW1

LIBRARY OF CONGRESS CATALOG CARD NUMBER: 76-187231

PRINTED IN THE UNITED STATES OF AMERICA

Contents

List of Contributors

Numbers in parentheses indicate the pages on which the authors' contributions begin.

JUSTIN ARONFREED, Department of Psychology, University of Pennsylvania, Philadelphia, Pennsylvania (93)

ALBERT BANDURA, Department of Psychology, Stanford University, Stanford, California (35)

J. ALLAN CHEYNE, Department of Psychology, University of Waterloo, Waterloo, Ontario, Canada (77)

BRIAN COATES, Department of Psychology, University of North Carolina, Chapel Hill, North Carolina (63)

JACOB L. GEWIRTZ, National Institute of Mental Health, National Institutes of Health, Bethesda, Maryland (7)

WILLARD W. HARTUP, Institute of Child Development, University of Minnesota, Minneapolis, Minnesota (63)

ROSS D. PARKE,* Department of Psychology, The University of Wisconsin, Madison, Wisconsin (1)

*Present address: The Fels Research Institute for the Study of Human Development, Yellow Springs, Ohio.

Preface

Research in the area of child psychology, particularly in social development in children, has changed rapidly in the past decade. One of the most influential and important positions in this area of child development has been social learning theory. Although there have been isolated chapters and papers on the shape and organization of thinking in this tradition, this volume offers a convenient overview of the current state of social learning theory. The papers were originally presented at a memorial symposium in honor of the late Richard H. Walters, one of the outstanding contributors to a social learning analysis of child development. This volume is part of that memorial tribute. It will be of interest to students and professionals in child development as well as in social and clinical psychology.

Six outstanding scholars, all active researchers in the field of social development, are represented. Gewirtz presents an up-to-date review of his theoretical views on the social reinforcement issue. Bandura and Hartup both offer current analyses of the imitation issue—a central concern of social learning theory. Bandura presents a summary of his contiguity theory of modeling, which emphasizes the important role played by symbolic coding processes in imitation. Hartup, on the other hand, argues cogently for a developmental analysis of imitation and points to new directions for future analyses of the problem. In another paper, Cheyne, a former collaborator of Walters, presents an empirical and theoretical overview of the current status of punishment and its role in the development of self-control in children. In the final paper, Aronfreed offers a cogent and lively discussion of the preceding contributions. I have written an introductory chapter which not only relates the papers to the work of R. H. Walters but underlines the recent theoretical trends represented by them as well.

In keeping with the memorial function of the collection, the proceeds from sales of the volume are being transferred to the R. H. Walters Memorial Award Fund at the University of Waterloo. Each year, the fund awards a cash prize to an outstanding student graduating from the honors psychology program at Waterloo.

I would like to thank the contributors for the thought and effort that went into transforming their papers from symposia presentations to their present form. Finally, thanks are extended to Frances Hall for her assistance in the typing and indexing of this volume.

Ross D. Parke*

*Present address: The Fels Research Institute for the Study of Human Development, Yellow Springs, Ohio.

chapter 1

Overview | *Ross D. Parke*

On March 26, 1969, the Society for Research in Child Development held a memorial symposium in honor of Richard H. Walters. The tribute was made in the form of a series of papers, presented by individuals invited to comment on the current status and future trends in the area of social learning theory. Before introducing these papers, a few remarks are in order about the man in whose honor they were written.

Richard H. Walters is best known for his theoretical contributions and his ingenious experimental investigations in the area of social learning. He was dissatisfied with traditional theorizing in child psychology and spent much of his professional career searching for a more satisfactory theoretical framework.

His principal theoretical contribution was, of course, *Social Learning and Personality Development* which he co-authored with Albert Bandura. This slim, but highly influential, volume provided a conceptual framework for a systematic application of learning-theory principles to the study of social development. But it was much more than an orthodox learning approach. Recognition was given to the central role that imitation and modeling play in the acquisition and modification of social behavior.

However, his theoretical analyses were not limited to that volume. In addition, he made a major contribution in the area of social reinforcement. In a series of experimental studies, Walters tried to demonstrate the futility of applying "drive" concepts to the analysis of social development. These studies resulted in the celebrated controversy between Gewirtz and

Walters over the interpretation of the effects of social deprivation on social reinforcers' effectiveness.

One of Walters' innovative theoretical contributions was his analysis of the role played by social judgments in our use of terms such as *dependency* and *aggression,* (Walters & Parke, 1964). According to this approach, the definition and classification of a social behavior involves a social judgment, such that behavior judged in one situation may be labeled aggressive or dependent, whereas the same behavior may be classified under a different label in another context or by a different observer. The implication of this analysis is that social learning theory should investigate how a child learns to make the social judgments that enable him to classify and label social behaviors. Walters was by no means an armchair theoretician and in a study with Brown (Walters & Brown, 1964), he experimentally demonstrated how social judgments affect our definition of aggressive behavior.

In addition to his contributions to social reinforcement, aggression, dependency, and imitation, in the later years of his career Walters conducted an extensive program of studies of the effects of punishment on children's social behavior. In part, he was eager to challenge the traditional view that punishment was an ineffective means of controlling human behavior. His careful empirical analysis of the parameters that alter the effectiveness of punishment clearly demonstrated the fallacy of this orthodox assumption (Walters & Parke, 1967). Furthermore, he was not satisfied with the ordinary interpretations of punishment. As Cheyne notes in his paper, Walters infused new life into this area by his emphasis on the role of cognitive and attentional factors in the operation of punishment.

At the final stage of his career, Walters was working on a new series of studies in comparative development—an examination of the effects of early rearing experiences on the development of social attachments in dogs. It was ironic that he met his death in the process of caring for a litter of newborn pups. In addition to the dog experiments, he was also examining the role of problem solving in cats and remarked that cats are not nearly as dull as Thorndike had imagined—you just have to train them properly or maybe show them an appropriate model. It is witness to his breadth that only some aspects of his wide range of interests are represented in the following papers.

In the first paper, Gewirtz has updated and restated the issues that were originally involved in the deprivation-satiation controversy over which he and Walters so vigorously fought. More importantly, he has placed the original "social deprivation" debate into a much broader perspective by viewing deprivation-satiation operations as simply one type of contextual factor that affects an individual's reactions to stimulus input. Not only are preceding conditions important in this analysis but concurrent factors are emphasized, as well. Gewirtz's emphasis on the physical and social ecology of the setting as determinants of stimulus effects is a timely reminder of an important, but often neglected, class of conditions. Dick Walters would have applauded, for up to the time of his death he was involved in a naturalistic ecological study of nursery school children.

In the next two papers, Bandura and Hartrup offer new views on imitation—an area to which Walters made substantial contributions. Bandura's paper represents a summary of the expanded contiguity view of imitation originally offered by Bandura and Walters in their 1963 book. In this analysis, the processes that must be considered in a "comprehensive theory of vicarious learning" are detailed: attention, retention, and motoric reproduction. Of particular interest and importance is the detailed analysis of the role of symbolic coding in modeling. It is clear from Bandura's paper that social learning approaches have benefited significantly from recent advances in human information processing. The somewhat cognitively barren framework that was characteristic of social learning theory is undergoing marked changes with increasing emphasis being given to the cognitive status and abilities of the organism.

In a final section of his presentation, Bandura offers evidence in favor of a discrimination interpretation of generalized imitation. However, the issue is still open, and the secondary reinforcement view originally offered by Baer and Sherman is still a viable alternative (Waxler & Yarrow, 1970).

Hartup presents a series of cogent arguments for a redirection of research emphasis in the area of imitation. Specifically, he suggests that a more developmental attack on the problem is necessary on the assumption that "imitation is intertwined with a variety of cognitive and motivational changes taking place during childhood." Not only are studies of imitation at different ages and stages of development required, but the origin of first imitations merits attention as well. In exploring the issue of early imitations, Hartup explicitly expands the range of possible influences to include innate factors—a class of variables too often given only passing recognition in social learning theory approaches. Hartup also points out that parental imitation of infant behavior may form the basis for the development of infant imitative responses. This is reminiscent of Bell's thesis (Bell, 1968) that children's responses often shape adult's behavior—a recognition that children as well as adults play *active* roles in the socialization process.

In the fourth paper, Cheyne discusses some of the final research efforts made by Walters in the area of punishment. This series of experimental studies illustrates not only that punishment is effective but also that an understanding of the manner in which punishment operates requires new approaches. The anxiety-based model that originally guided this research is only partly correct; Cognitive and attentional factors clearly merit consideration in analyzing punishment's role in the development of self-control. In line with emphases in other parts of the social learning enterprise, Cheyne gives developmental factors their due. Specifically, he demonstrates that cognitive variables may play an increasingly important role in the development of response inhibition as the child matures.

A final aspect of this program merits underlining, namely, the use of psychophysiological indices as an aid to interpreting social psychological data. Walters was one of the first to demonstrate the usefulness of this approach to understanding social development (Walters, 1968).

In the final paper in this series, Aronfreed lucidly summarizes the comments and suggestions that he offered at the symposium in his role as discussant. It is the sign of a healthy and lively area that is marked by controversy, disagreement, and debate. If Aronfreed's remarks can be used as a basis for a prognosis, then the field is clearly alive and well!

In conclusion, these papers will indeed serve their memorial function most appropriately if they stimulate further research. It is clear that this is the kind of tribute that would have pleased the man these papers are honoring—Richard Haig Walters.

REFERENCES

Bandura, A., & Walters, R. H. *Social Learning and Personality Development.* New York: 1963.

Bell, R. Q. A reinterpretation of the direction of effects of socialization. *Psychological Review,* 1968, 75, 81-95.

Walters, R. H. The effects of social isolation and social interaction on learning and performance in social situations. In D. C. Glass (Ed.) *Environmental Influences*. New York: Rockefeller Univ. Press, 1968. Pp. 155-184.

Walters, R. H., & Brown, M. A test of the high-magnitude theory of aggression. *Journal of Experimental Child Psychology,* 1964, **1,** 376-387.

Walters, R. H., & Parke, R. D. Social motivation, dependency, and susceptibility to social influence. In L. Berkowitz (Ed.), *Advances in experimental social psychology.* Vol. I. New York: Academic Press, 1964. Pp. 231-276.

Walters, R. H., & Parke, R. D. The influence of punishment and related disciplinary techniques on the social behavior of children. In B. A. Maher (Ed.), *Progress in experimental personality research.* Vol. IV. New York: Academic Press, 1967. Pp. 179-228.

Waxler, C. Z., & Yarrow, M. R. Factors influencing imitative learning in preschool children. *Journal of Experimental Child Psychology,* 1970, **9,** 115-130.

chapter 2

Some Contextual Determinants of Stimulus Potency[1] | *Jacob L. Gewirtz*

Although I had previously met Richard Walters, we did not actually make scientific contact until 1960, when he published the first of a series of studies on social isolation and anxiety as determinants of social-reinforcer efficacy. In those early studies Dick disputed the working assumption underlying some experiments reported a few years earlier by Donald Baer and me. Specifically, he questioned that the treatment condition of brief social isolation (that Baer and I found expedient to implement in our work) actually represented a condition of "social deprivation" that operated orthogonally to "anxiety," as we had assumed. Dick's interpretation

[1] The author of this paper wishes to thank Laura Rosenthal and Danielle Spiegler for their dedicated editorial assistance and constructive suggestions in the preparation of this report. Dr. Donald M. Baer's suggestions helped to improve an early version of this paper. The opinions expressed herein are those of the author and do not necessarily represent the position of the National Institute of Mental Health.

was that the effects we found were due to "anxiety" rather than to deprivation. And so he and several of his students proceeded to mount a series of experiments in an attempt to show that some condition of "anxiety" (and after 1964, of "arousal") was the prime determinant of the behavior-rate increases that resulted from the brief social-isolation condition. Thus began almost a decade of stimulating interaction between us. Through those years, Dick and I drew intellectually and personally close, coming to see a number of issues in similar ways and clarifying our differences on others.

Our last major conceptual confrontation took place in a symposium debate at the 1965 biennial meeting of the Society for Research in Child Development. At that time, Dick modified his anxiety-arousal interpretation of social isolation and articulately tied in his conception with a systematic social-learning approach to noxious stimulation and its consequences. At the same time, I presented a preliminary report of some experiments I had undertaken using a relative-satiation design for a single stimulus class *without* the use of a brief isolation condition. This new design permitted the detection of deprivation effects in a way that precluded the interpretation of the results as possibly being due to conditions ordinarily termed "frustration," "anxiety," or "arousal." At that point, it seemed that Dick and I might no longer be focusing on the very same problem, that our continuing debate might no longer be functional, and that we might savor its recollection as history.

Many in this audience will recall the legend that inspired Anatole France's "Le Jongleur de Notre Dame." The tale relates back to medieval times when the faithful paid homage to a likeness of the Virgin with gifts that both the religious and secular worlds valued. An impoverished juggler paid tribute to the Virgin in the one way he could: Using his only currency, he juggled for Our Lady! I can do no better than that juggler now. In the same spirit, I would like to pay homage to the memory of Richard Haig Walters, that most intelligent, creative, exuberant, vigorous, earthy, broth of a man, who contributed so much, in but one decade, to theory and research on social behavior and learning, and whose passing cut short such an exemplary career. I shall do this in a way I think Dick would have wanted it: By continuing the direction of our last debate, in which we attempted to understand the bases and dimensionalities of *Some Contextual Determinants of Stimulus Potency.*

INTRODUCTION

The *effectiveness* of a stimulus in controlling an individual's behavior on a particular occasion, by evoking, cueing, or reinforcing it, is typically dependent upon the contextual features of stimulus provision and may be enhanced or decreased by their manipulation. Indeed, even the *direction-ality* of a stimulus may be determined by the context of its provision. Some of the more familiar contextual conditions involve the deprivation or satiation of appetitive stimuli. Others involve the many types of background conditions that are present when a stimulus (figure) is pro-vided. These are frequently varied systematically in perceptual research but may be neglected in behavioral analyses. Thus, although the evocative, discriminative, and reinforcing stimuli that are manipulated in condi-tioning experiments are generally described in sufficient detail, the often-controlled contextual setting conditions that may be critical determinants of their efficacy are not always made explicit. This paper will survey a variety of these contextual conditions, particularly those that are relevant for child behavior systems.

It would be unnecessary to consider the context of stimulus pro-vision if successive presentations of a stimulus were to lead consistently to the same response. However, this homogeneity in responding is rare, and it is therefore important to consider the conditions under which a stimulus has a certain impact on behavior. Many of these momentary factors have been labeled, and frequently attributed gratuitously to, "drives" or "states" of the organism at the time of stimulation (e.g., Helson, 1959), but because of the often ambiguous or excess meanings of such motiva-tional terms, some researchers have preferred to call them "setting" conditions (e.g., Bijou & Baer, 1963; Gewirtz, 1967, 1969a; Kantor, 1959). Contextual conditions have also often been termed "performance" factors to separate them from those of "learning." Once the relevant contextual setting conditions have been identified, and the functions that relate those conditions, the focal stimulus, and the response have been specified, the use of "drive" or "state" terms would be superfluous for many purposes.

Contextual conditions that affect the salience of a stimulus for an individual's behavior may be grouped according to their temporal relationship to the stimulus being presented, that is, the focal stimulus. Contextual qualifiers may operate either concurrently with or preceding the presentation of the focal stimulus, and their effects may cumulate. Examples of concurrent qualifiers are the ground for a stimulus figure, the agency of reinforcement, and a standard or anchor stimulus.[2] Examples of preceding qualifiers include a cue to where the focal stimulus will appear, an instructional or training set, stimulus deprivation-satiation contexts, a previous pattern of contingent focal stimulus presentation, and earlier judgments by others of some stimulus attribute.

The categories used here to classify the diverse contextual factors are gross and preliminary. Contextual qualifiers, particularly those that operate prior to presentations of the focal stimulus, could be ordered along so many dimensions that the classifications used in this analysis inevitably overlap. Some of the concurrent or preceding contextual qualifiers of stimulus efficacy will readily be interpretable as outcomes of learning (e.g., the conditioned value of a particular reinforcement source, facilitating or constraining preparatory sets). Others do not appear to have been established through learning at all (e.g., the deprivation-satiation context for a stimulus) but may be qualified by longer-term experiential patterns that conceivably involve forms of learning as yet poorly defined, for example, those patterns that come to comprise an individual's adaptation or maintenance level, or "schema," for a stimulus class.

The discussion that follows will not deal with the process by which a stimulus acquires its value for behavior. Rather, it assumes that such value has already been acquired and is being maintained in the wider environmental context (for instance, by appropriate pairing conditions in the case of a conditioned reinforcer). The acquisition process is therefore of secondary interest here, except that we recognize that contextual setting operations can facilitate that acquisition. Thus, this paper will deal only with the effect of contextual qualifiers on the efficacy of an already functional stimulus.

[2] Helson (e.g., 1959) appears to have restricted the term "contextual stimuli" to "background" or concurrent factors operating on focal stimuli. He appears to classify "organic states," the organism's past experience, and constitutional features as "residual" factors. However, in terms of our classification both types of factors would be included under the general heading of contextual stimuli.

SOME CONTEXTUAL QUALIFIERS

Concurrent Contextual Conditions

The effect on stimulus efficacy of setting conditions that operate concurrently with the focal stimulus may be illustrated by research examples from several different areas of psychology. In paired-associate learning, change of background color has been found to decrease the recall of syllables (Dulsky, 1935; Weiss & Margolius, 1954). In psychophysics, the concurrent presence of an anchor stimulus will characteristically affect judgments of stimulus attributes (Helson, 1964). Further, characteristics of the individual (which are presumed outcomes of learning) can constitute a framework to qualify the potency of a stimulus. Thus, after positive verbal reinforcement, more children with low levels of aspiration raised their expectancies of success than did children with high aspiration levels (Crandall, Good, & Crandall, 1964).

There is also considerable evidence that the discriminative or reinforcing value of a stimulus may be qualified by various *attributes of the source* of that stimulus, including the source's gender, social or role status, popularity, or even spatial orientation and occupation relative to the child subject. In a number of studies, reinforcing stimuli dispensed by an adult are found to be more effective in altering the behavior of a child of the opposite gender rather than of the same gender (Gewirtz, 1954; Gewirtz & Baer, 1958a, 1958b; Patterson, Littman, & Hinsey, 1964). Similarly, the effectiveness of a verbal reinforcer for child behavior has been found to be inversely related both to the child's liking for the peer reinforcing agent (Hartup, 1964) and to that agent's sociometric popularity (Tiktin & Hartup, 1965). Further, an adult's presence can evoke a greater number of attention-seeking and similar social responses from young children when the adult is busy and distant than when attentive and near (Gewirtz, 1954). Moreover, the frequency of a child's dominant behaviors depended on the behaviors of the person with whom he was in interaction—that is, his dominant behaviors increased in incidence when he was paired with the less assertive of two peers (Gellert, 1962). Some research and speculations about the role of contextual characteristics of socializing agents in the modification of child behavior are reported by Patterson (1969). Insofar as such stimulus characteristics may involve learning, they are considered more fully in the section on contextual conditions that precede the presentation of a focal stimulus.

The opportunities that stimuli can provide for behavior and learning are also affected by the physical and social ecology of a setting. As used here, the term "ecology" stands for the gross conditions of an environment that determine which events and behaviors can occur in a situation and, specifically, whether or not a child can receive a stimulus or emit a response. In this sense, such facilitators or constraints may be classified as contextual setting conditions. The amount of floor space available, positions of walls and of furniture, and props represent *physical* conditions that can grossly facilitate or constrain behavior systems. Similarly, the explicit and implicit rules and regulations in a setting as well as the type and number of peers and adults available there represent *social* facilitators or constraints on behavior systems. Thus, ecological conditions can insulate a child against, or cause him to be exposed to, various adults, children, and their specific activities, thereby determining the likelihood that the child will have the opportunity to receive certain stimuli, to emit particular responses, and to be reinforced for those responses (Gewirtz, 1968a, 1969a, 1971a, 1971c, 1972). Such potential ecological effects on behavior have up to now received too little emphasis in theoretical or research approaches to child-behavior systems.

Preceding Contextual Conditions

Stimulus functioning, and even the setting conditions which operate concurrently with the stimulus, may often be affected by *preceding* contextual conditions of stimulus provision. It has long been known in psychophysics that an individual's response to a stimulus will depend on his *history of stimulation,* that is, the type and range of stimuli to which he has been exposed (cf., e.g., Delboeuf, 1873, as quoted by Stevens, 1958). The shift of an individual's psychophysical judgments of stimuli toward the mean value of the stimulus series presented has been termed the "central-tendency effect" and characterized as the "relativity of judgment" (Stevens, 1958). Thus, when presented with a range of test stimuli, individuals' judgments of "same as" will be displaced in the direction of the central stimulus value to which they are earlier exposed (Helson &

Avant, 1967). Further, individuals will systematically assign different psychophysical-scale values to a standard shock stimulus depending on the average level of previously experienced shock intensities (Bevan & Adamson, 1960). And the accuracy of length judgments by individual adult subjects made in a group context may be decreased in the direction of the incorrect judgments earlier made there by confederates of the experimenter (Asch, 1952).

Instructional sets that direct an organism either to relevant features of a stimulus array or to a response task can also determine the efficacy of a stimulus for behavior. Thus, in a discrimination learning task, instructions to children to orient toward a reinforcing stimulus lessened the detrimental effects of delay in reinforcer receipt (Fagan & Witryol, 1966). In addition, more risk-taking responses were made by subjects given risk-oriented instructions than by those given neutral instructions, with the two instructional sets differing in but a single word (Clark & Willems, 1969). And, it has long been known that instructions can determine the potency of a stimulus in classical conditioning, as indicated, for instance, by response acquisition rate (Hilgard & Humphries, 1938; Kimble, 1961).

Earlier conditioning experiences of an individual may also modify the potency of a stimulus at any given moment. Such prior experience may operate in various ways, in both classical and instrumental conditioning. For example, repeated acquisition and extinction can increase the rapidity of subsequent conditioning (Brogden, Lipman, & Culler, 1938; Bullock & Smith, 1953) and of discrimination reversals (Dufort, Guttman, & Kimble, 1954). Similarly, subjects of various species given a series of discrimination problems have shown improvement both in rate of responding and in number of errors. This process has been termed a "learning set" or "learning-to-learn" (Harlow, 1959).

Prior experience with a stimulus source may also determine stimulus efficacy for behavior. An agent may routinely have been the source only of positive reinforcement, only of aversive stimulation, or of both stimulus types; or during a single prior treatment session an experimenter may have provided the child with positive, negative, or neutral interaction. These prior conditions can qualify the efficacy for the child's behavior of both positive and negative stimuli from that source. For instance, positive reinforcers (McCoy & Zigler, 1965) and negative reinforcers (Parke & Walters, 1967) were each more effective for children after sessions of positive interaction than after sessions of neutral or impersonal contact with an experimenter. However, positive reinforcers from an experimenter were more powerful after a negative than after a positive interaction with him (Berkowitz, Butterfield, & Zigler, 1965). Also pertinent here are the findings that (1) social reinforcers (connoting approval) from an experimenter were more effective after a session in which attention was first provided and then withdrawn than after a session of continuous attention (Hartup, 1958), and (2) an experimenter's prohibition was more effective for children left alone after an attention-withdrawal condition than after a session of constant attentive interaction (Parke, 1967).

Earlier patterns of reinforcement magnitude or rate can also qualify the efficacy of such stimuli in instrumental conditioning (Black, 1968; Dunham, 1968). Thus, the stimulus-contingency pattern comprising an earlier reinforcement schedule can control the response pattern and rate under the same stimuli comprising a subsequent schedule (e.g., Weiner, 1969a, 1969b; Weisberg, 1970). For example, Weiner found that human adults initially conditioned under fixed-ratio reinforcement that generated a high, constant response rate exhibited similar high rates under subsequent fixed- and variable-interval reinforcement schedules, even though these latter schedules would ordinarily generate low response rates. Similarly, components of a multiple schedule of reinforcement can interact so that the pattern of stimulus provision under one component will determine the behavior rate under another. Thus, in a multiple schedule, the response rate maintained by a standard rate of reinforcement in the presence of a particular discriminative stimulus can be changed by altering the reinforcement rate maintaining that response in the presence of a different discriminative stimulus: It can be increased when combined (i.e., contrasted) with a denser schedule and decreased when combined with a sparser schedule (e.g., Brethower & Reynolds, 1962; Herrnstein & Brady, 1958; Reynolds, 1961a, 191b; Terrace, 1966). (The opposite will hold for negative reinforcement.) It has recently been shown that such behavioral-contrast effects can be produced in rats even when two very different responses are involved, when there are marked differences between the two reinforcing events, or when the time interval between the two discriminative occasions is greatly extended (Premack, 1969).

Even the effectiveness of *stimuli of inherently high salience* can be qualified, although it has generally been assumed that such stimulus effects are not readily susceptible to modification. For instance, Bevan and Adamson (1960) modified the reinforcing efficacy of a cutaneous electric shock for human adults by earlier subjecting them to different intensity distributions and average levels of shock. On the other hand, an otherwise trivial event may be made to function as a potent discriminative or reinforcing stimulus for behavior if the contextual aspects of the environment are considered and properly manipulated. For example, in a test situation in which an achievement-oriented child might wish to please a prestigious tester-experimenter, almost any trivial but systematic response by that experimenter, such as his clicking a ballpoint pen or clearing his throat, might function as an effective discriminative or reinforcing stimulus for that child's behavior. All too frequently such contextual conditions that qualify or determine the functional effectiveness of stimuli are only implied in reports of conditioning experiments with children. However, if we are to understand how the potential discriminative or reinforcing stimuli can be made to function effectively and uniformly, particularly in social situations, the operation of contextual setting conditions in an investigation must be reported in appropriate detail.

Deprivation and *satiation* for a stimulus can also illustrate how context conditions can operate (through hours or days) preceding the presentation of a stimulus to qualify its potency on a particular occasion. Deprivation of a stimulus refers to its removal, or to a decrease in the rate of its provision, leading to an increase in its effectiveness; and satiation for a stimulus refers to its repeated presentation, or an increase in the rate of its provision, leading to a decrease in its effectiveness. *Recovery* from satiation, which involves an increase in stimulus efficacy brought about by a period (following satiation) during which the stimulus is not provided, is thereby the conceptual equivalent of deprivation. The reinforcing potency of a stimulus (the typical stimulus role used in deprivation-satiation studies) will thus be a direct function of the degree of the organism's deprivation for it at that particular moment, usually indexed by the length of time that the stimulus has been withheld.

Traditionally, deprivation-satiation functions had been thought to hold uniquely for organismic "needs" and had been studied primarily with regard to food and water. In recent years, however, deprivation and satiation relationships have also been found to function in diverse species for the reinforcing potency of various *non*appetitive stimuli, such as visual and auditory events (e.g., Butler, 1957; Fox, 1962; Jones, 1964; Jones, Wilkinson, & Braden, 1961; Kish, 1966; Odom, 1964). Further, when deprivation is combined with some other type of setting condition, the effects on stimulus potency of the two conditions may be additive. Thus, information reinforcement was found to be more effective in maintaining the responding of adults who were deprived of information when they were also either deprived of food *or* subjected to occasional (noncontingent) electric shocks than when they were only deprived of information (Jones, 1961).

Functions comparable to those for deprivation-satiation, but that have involved primarily the *evocative* or *discriminative* (rather than the reinforcing) roles of visual, auditory, and tactile stimuli, have been classified under *curiosity, manipulation* and *investigation*, stimulus *familiarity-novelty* and *complexity,* and *play,* as well as *attention* and *vigilance* (Beach, 1945; Berlyne, 1950, 1955, 1957, 1960; Dember & Earl, 1957; Glanzer, 1953, 1958; Kish, 1966; Montgomery, 1953; Welker, 1956). Comparable functions for the evocative role of stimuli have also been grouped under the headings of short-term response *adaptation* or *habituation.* Under these latter headings, systematic decrements in (for the most part) seemingly unconditioned responses have often been identified as a function of exposure to a stimulus, or to successive stimuli. Recovery in response strength is implemented after a time period during which the stimulus(i) is not presented (and the response does not occur), or sometimes by the introduction of a (novel) stimulus not recently (or ever) presented (e.g., Berlyne, 1957; Bevan, 1965; Cantor, 1968; Cantor & Cantor, 1964, 1965, 1966; Cook & Vachon, 1968; Endsley, 1967; Gullickson, 1966; Harris, 1965; Hinde, 1954, 1960; Mendel, 1965). In this connection, we note that the greater the habituation of responses (psychophysiological or behavioral) connoting the *orienting reflex* (and hence attention) to novel stimuli before Pavlovian conditioning, the more difficult it is to establish a conditioned reflex to one of those stimuli (Maltzman, 1968; Sokolov, 1963). Thus, the magnitude of a *GSR* index of the orienting reflex to the first presentation of a (to-be-conditioned) stimulus varied inversely with the number of prior presentations of similar stimuli (Wolff & Maltzman, 1968). However, orienting reflex habituation as an explanation for the loss of stimulus efficacy only substitutes one set of functional relations for another. Therefore, the functional relations denoting systematic decreases in stimulus efficacy as a function of stimulus presentations could stand independently as descriptive explanations of the process.

Functional relations connoting deprivation-satiation have similarly been identified for *social* stimuli (Bacon & Stanley, 1963; Gewirtz & Baer, 1958a, 1958b; Gewirtz, Baer, & Roth, 1958). Gewirtz and Baer (1958a, 1958b) reported that the reinforcing effectiveness of a class of spoken words connoting approval (e.g., *good, fine*) in a discrimination-learning task with young children was enhanced when immediately preceded by 20 minutes of social isolation (conceptualized as relative deprivation of the stimulus used), and it was lowered when preceded by 20 minutes in which the stimulus class was provided in relative abundance (conceptualized as relative satiation). Further, we reported that brief social isolation increased the reinforcing efficacy of words connoting adult approval for preschool children in direct proportion to the degree to which those children's behavior was rated as being characteristically maintained by adult approval in other settings (a finding that is consonant with the maintenance-level conception to be discussed in a later section) (Gewirtz & Baer, 1958b).

The basic relationship identified by Gewirtz and Baer, involving the differential effect of brief social isolation on social reinforcement, has been replicated and extended in similar experiments with human subjects of various ages (Dorwart, Ezerman, Lewis, & Rosenhan, 1965; Endo, 1968; Erickson, 1962; Gallimore, Tharp, & Kemp, 1969; Hill & Stevenson, 1964; Kozma, 1969; Lewis, 1965; Lewis & Richman, 1964; Rosenhan, 1967; Stevenson & Odom, 1961, 1962; Walters & Ray, 1960; for a wide-ranging survey of these and related findings, see Eisenberger, 1970). However, the interpretation of this almost homogeneous array of results as due to the operation of deprivation and satiation has been questioned by some theorists, who have proposed alternative explanations: "sensory deprivation" (Walters & Quinn, 1960); dependency "frustration" and/or "anxiety" (Walters & Ray, 1960); "arousal" (Walters & Parke, 1964) (arousal and anxiety apparently differing in name only); and "frustration" which might manifest itself in aggressive behaviors under other conditions

(Hartup & Himeno, 1959). We recall that in our first study Baer and I noted the possibility of these alternative interpretations of the mechanism underlying our social isolation operations (Gewirtz & Baer, 1958b, p. 53). Although our experimental design did not permit us to rule out these interpretations definitively, we thought the operation of such factors to be unlikely and, in any event, conceived that they would operate orthogonally to deprivation-satiation operations.

Nevertheless, to provide an empirical basis for precluding such interpretations and to determine a deprivation-satiation relationship for a *single* social stimulus class without directly affecting the availability of any other stimuli, some experiments using a relative-satiation and recovery design *without* the use of an isolation condition were undertaken by Gewirtz (1967, 1969b) and by Landau and Gewirtz (1967). These studies illustrated how stimulus satiation and deprivation can determine the reinforcing potency of a social stimulus, the word *good* (or the comparable Hebrew word *yafeh*) connoting approval, in the discrimination-learning of young boys. The reinforcing efficacy of the social stimulus dispensed by a woman[3] was found (1) to vary inversely with the number of prior contin-

---

[3] As in most experimental paradigms, there is often the problem in deprivation-satiation studies that the conditions of stimulus provision are potentially confounded by experimenter bias. Having different experimenters serve in treatment and test phases of an experiment is sometimes used as a control, but should not be considered a solution in studies of this nature. The characteristics of the experimenter are assumed to be an important part of the stimulus complex, and employing different experimenters in the two phases might change this stimulus complex enough to attenuate and make undetectable the underlying relationship between relative deprivation-satiation conditions and stimulus efficacy. Indeed, this is one possible basis for the failure of McArthur and Zigler (1969) to replicate the results of Gewirtz's relative satiation studies. Another possible control for experimenter bias could be to use a naive experimenter for both treatment and test, but this solution would be inadequate also to the extent that it could be assumed that experimenters always have some theory about the outcomes expected and, in principle, could bias them in the direction of their particular theory. For this same reason, employing many experimenters (even if they were to produce homogeneous results) would not in itself insure against bias.

In this context, even though several replications of the experimental design with the stimulus word *good* have yielded homogeneous outcomes, it would seem best to replicate the design with diverse stimuli, whose values have been acquired on various bases, some of which function in other than reinforcing roles. This list should include particularly stimuli programmed and presented by nonsocial sources. Indeed, an ordinarily nonsocial stimulus (such as a nonaversive sound or light of short

gent or noncontingent stimulus presentations to the child (i.e., the degree of his satiation for the stimulus), and (2) to vary directly with the length of recovery interval between satiation treatment and learning test.

In the Gewirtz and Baer study reported earlier, satiation and recovery for social stimuli were found to produce opposite, seemingly additive, effects like those which characterize satiation and recovery (i.e., deprivation) functions for appetitive stimuli. Although we thought it gratuitous to apply the term "social drive" to such functional relations, as has often been done, we used the term to provide historical context for our results. We subsequently regretted this action, as our original purpose has frequently been misinterpreted. Having identified a dimension of contextual setting conditions, the description of the functional relation is sufficient for most requirements.

Some contextual setting conditions may uniquely affect the potency of one stimulus, and other contextual conditions may affect the values for behavior of a wide range of stimuli. If depriving or satiating an organism for a specific stimulus were found to change the behavioral effects of several other stimuli as well, the operation might be interpreted under some theoretical approaches as increasing or decreasing the organism's level of "arousal," "anxiety," or "general drive" (or as involving the concurrent habituation of responses to stimuli which connote the orienting reflex). Even so, the functional relation between the reinforcing efficacy of a stimulus and its prior satiation or recovery can stand independently of such concepts as general drive or arousal or even the habituation of orientation responses, just as they often do in deprivation-satiation relations involving appetitive stimuli.

MAINTENANCE CONDITIONS AS
STIMULUS CONTEXTS

There is considerable evidence that the pattern of an individual's long-term experience with a stimulus can affect its momentary efficacy

---

duration) might be dispensed homogeneously by a mechanical device in a nonsocial experimental session, and could be given social connotation (like approval or achievement) by implementing a relevant setting condition prior to the session. Programming the provision of stimuli in this way, therefore, would go far to preclude the possibility of experimenter bias. It could also provide a test of the sometimes-advanced notion (thought by the writer to be incorrect) that there is a functional difference between social and nonsocial stimuli.

for behaviors. Therefore, a discussion of maintenance levels or reference standards and of discrepancy or incongruity hypotheses is pertinent here. I have noted in an earlier section that, beginning with early psychophysics, a considerable literature has accrued on the "relativity of judgment" that is sometimes termed "normative adaptation" or "frame-of-reference" psychophysics (Bevan, 1965; Stevens, 1958). Specifically, it appears that the distributional characteristics ("levels") of an individual's pattern of experience with a stimulus may somehow come to function as reference standards to determine the efficacy for his behavior of an implemented level (or combination of elements) of the stimulus, even including those related to basic organismic requirements. These often long-term maintenance patterns can be indexed by distributional features such as the number, variety, and range of types, or average rate or intensity level, of stimulus values experienced. Thus, an individual may respond more readily to a stimulus level that is close to the average level previously experienced than to an extreme, infrequently experienced value of that stimulus; or he may respond in a manner that will maintain the previous (adaptation) level of stimulation and avoid the highly infrequent ("incongruent") level. Moreover, some have assumed that maximal stimulus efficacy will result when the discrepancy between that stimulus and its maintenance-level standard is in the intermediate range.

Perhaps the most notable example of a stimulation-level summarizing concept is Helson's (1947, 1948, 1959, 1964) "adaptation level." Helson has described how the weighted geometric average of focal, background, and residual stimuli earlier experienced by the individual can function as a "frame of reference" (standard, context) for diverse stimulus-response systems, to qualify the impact on behavior of a subsequently presented stimulus. As each new stimulus is presented, its characteristics are incorporated into the individual's pattern of experience, and his adaptation level changes accordingly.

A very similar conception of seemingly learned maintenance levels or reference standards is that they may serve to define the "familiar" for the individual, as a baselevel for responding to "novel," "incongruent," or "strange" stimuli. In this frame, Hebb (1946, 1949, 1966) has proposed that visual stimuli containing elements very incongruent with those the individual has previously experienced (and presumably "encoded") might evoke emotional behaviors leading to avoidance or uncoordinated excitement, whereas stimuli containing more congruent, but still different, elements might evoke curiosity and investigatory behaviors. For instance, chimpanzees typically displayed strong fear responses when presented with stimuli that were atypical in terms of previous maintenance contexts (e.g., the inert body of an anesthetized chimpanzee or a chimpanzee skull with moving jaw) (Hebb, 1946). And in human infants, an intermediate level of incongruence of a stimulus from a set of values regularly experienced earlier (an encoded "stimulus schema") resulted in an increased duration of responses connoting attention (Lewis & Goldberg, 1969; McCall & Kagan, 1967).

The general conception that stimulus function may be qualified by reference standards or adaptation levels appears to underlie diverse research programs (e.g., Bevan & Adamson, 1960, 1963; Lockard, 1962, 1964; Premack & Collier, 1962) and various theoretical approaches (e.g., McClelland, Atkinson, Clark, & Lowell, 1953, pp. 6-96). Similar notions have also been used by Glanzer (1958), Gewirtz (1961, 1967, 1968b), and Baron (1966), among others. For instance, Bevan and Adamson (1960, 1963) have proposed that the reinforcing efficacy of a stimulus presented on a particular occasion is a function of the discrepancy between its value and the adaptation level. Thus, as already noted, they have demonstrated that even the reinforcing efficacy of a stimulus of inherently high salience (a cutaneous electric shock of intermediate intensity) can be qualified for human adults by earlier subjecting them to different intensity distributions and average levels of the shock stimulus. Specifically, the reinforcing effectiveness of a standard shock in a learning task was an inverse function of the intensity of the shock level earlier repeatedly presented. In the same vein, Gewirtz, Jones, and Waerneryd (1956) found that adults' generalization-discrimination response gradients for visual-angle stimuli within a particular range were displaced in the direction of the (different) range of stimuli to which they had earlier responded.

If the momentary efficacy of a stimulus may be qualified by an individual's long-term maintenance pattern (level) for the stimulus class, then it is conceivable that such reference standards would also qualify the deprivation-satiation functions for food and diverse other stimuli. Thus, 18 hours without food might operate as a relative *deprivation* condition for organisms routinely fed more frequently (e.g., every 12 hours) and as a relative *satiation* condition for organisms regularly fed less frequently (e.g., every 24 hours). I have noted elsewhere that such a result might constitute a paradox under some conceptions of stimulus functioning or of drive conditions (Gewirtz, 1968b).

It therefore appears that, through some as yet inadequately identified process, facets of the stimulus maintenance pattern the organism has experienced (e.g., the classes, frequencies, rates, and/or ranges of stimuli received) can come to control his behavior as reference standards. Although the acquisition of a maintenance or adaptation level reflects experience and must therefore involve what would ordinarily be termed a "learning process," few proponents of molar conceptions of reference standards have speculated about possible learning mechanisms. An early task will be to investigate systematically how reference standards for stimulation are acquired, to determine how, if at all, the acquisition patterns fit the extant learning paradigms. Although many approaches contain terms such as "novelty" and "strangeness," the meaning and usefulness of which depend on the acquisition of background contexts that reflect patterns of stimulation experienced, there is as yet no approach that adequately accounts for their control over behaviors (approach or avoidance). However, if we are to gain a better understanding of behavioral development, these contextual factors and their acquisition bases must certainly be considered and incorporated into conceptions about the outcomes of early experience.

CONTEXT AND STIMULUS DIRECTIONALITY

There has been increasing evidence that a wide range of events can function with stimulus properties *opposite* to those ordinarily expected, depending on the context provided by concurrent or preceding conditions of stimulus provision. That is, in addition to affecting the cueing and reinforcing salience of a stimulus, the context of stimulus provision can also determine the *directionality* of effects of a stimulus, for instance, whether it will function as a positive reinforcer, a negative reinforcer, or have no value at all for behavior. Thus, the absence of any reaction from an adult experimenter can function as a positive reinforcing condition for children given negative verbal reinforcement during an earlier session, and as a negative reinforcing condition for children earlier given positive reinforcers (Crandall, Good, & Crandall, 1964). Further, after children have experienced success in an earlier task, the presence of supportive statements can function as positive reinforcement to improve their performance in a marble-insertion task, whereas after an earlier failure their performance can be lower under the presence of supportive statements than under nonreinforcement (Stevenson & Hill, 1965).

In addition, the same events that are nonfunctional for the satiated organism can function as positive reinforcers after they have been unavailable for a sufficient period, and as negative reinforcers when the satiated organism cannot avoid receiving them (as through forced feeding). Therefore, although it is routine to consider that certain stimuli are positive reinforcers (e.g., food or social events connoting approval or attention), most such stimuli function in this role only within a narrow range of conditions, for instance when the organism for whom they can function as stimuli has recovered from being satiated for them (i.e., after having been deprived of them). Indeed, if an infant is satiated for any stimulus which ordinarily functions as a positive reinforcer, he may then find such a stimulus aversive, whether it be food, light, sound, or a cutaneous or social event (Gewirtz, 1961, 1967, 1971b, 1971c). Conversely, for an infant limited in receiving what, for him, is a positive reinforcing stimulus, a normally aversive stimulus may function as a positive reinforcer. For instance, stimuli connoting "negative attention" from parents (via scolding) may positively reinforce a child's behavior after a period in which he has been ignored by them, especially if he ordinarily receives their attention. In this connection, Gallimore, Tharp, and Kemp (1969) found that, after a brief period of social isolation, children for whom social approval had strong positive reinforcing value (as determined by a questionnaire) emitted relatively more incorrect responses that were followed by "negative attention" (hearing the visible experimenter say "you're wrong") than correct responses that were followed by a light flash.

Further, stimuli that ordinarily function as positive or as negative reinforcers may do so only within a limited range of intensity values. Thus, stimulus events like electric shock which normally function as aversive stimuli at high intensities may function as positive reinforcers ("tingling sensations") at low intensities. In addition, a generally strong noxious stimulus can function like a positive reinforcer for behavior in a context in which an organism has to respond and must choose between a response followed by that stimulus and one followed by an even more noxious stimulus. For instance, human adults self-administered electric shocks in a context in which such responding could prevent a more severe electric shock (from an "aggressive" partner) (Stone & Hokanson, 1969). Moreover, the opportunity for an organism to respond can function like a positive reinforcer when made contingent upon another of his responses that characteristically occurs at a lower rate and, conversely, like a negative reinforcer when made contingent upon another response that characteristically occurs at a higher rate (Premack, 1959, 1962; Weisman & Premack, 1966).

Thus, knowledge of such contextual conditions could enable the advance specification of the reinforcement efficacy of a given stimulus as well as of the direction of its effects on behavior. In addition, it could permit the advance specification of the potential reinforcement value of the occurrence of particular responses, including which response of a pair will reinforce the other in a given situation. In this frame, speculation as to whether stimuli that ordinarily function as negative reinforcers are more or less potent than stimuli that usually function as positive reinforcers, or have different emotional behavior concomitants, would be of limited usefulness when approached as a general case (Gewirtz, 1971b, 1971c).

SUMMARY AND CONCLUSIONS

This paper has surveyed a variety of contextual setting conditions that can qualify the momentary efficacy, and even the direction of effects, of a (focal) stimulus in evoking, cueing, or reinforcing behavior. It would be unnecessary to consider the contextual factors of stimulus provision if repeated presentations of a stimulus were to lead consistently to the same response. However, such homogeneity is rare, particularly in social contexts. If, on a particular occasion, appropriate context conditions are not manipulated to make an event *relevant* for an organism, it may not exert optimal, or even effective, stimulus control over his behavior. Moreover, when such factors are unrecognized in a situation, they may operate to attenuate or even nullify the effects of a training program, or may even lead to artifactual outcomes.

Contextual factors were classified in this survey according to their temporal relation to focal stimulus functioning. However, we noted that this gross classification serves merely as a preliminary vehicle for listing the diverse phenomena that may operate to qualify stimulus efficacy. The categories almost routinely overlap, and their effects may be additive. Some contextual determinants do not appear to involve learning, some may be readily interpreted as the outcomes of learning, whereas others may be qualified by longer-term experiential conditions that seem to involve forms of learning as yet poorly understood. Under the heading of *concurrent* factors, we considered the ground for a stimulus figure, a standard or anchor stimulus, the source of reinforcing stimuli, and ecological factors that may facilitate or constrain responding. We then considered as contextual conditions that *precede* focal stimulus presentation those factors grouped under the headings of deprivation-satiation, curiosity, novelty, and habituation, instructional sets, earlier experience with stimulus attributes (including earlier judgments of stimulus attributes and serial position), and an organism's learning history (including earlier patterns of experience with a reinforcing agency or of focal stimulus presentation, and orienting sets established via learning procedures). Insofar as these latter factors may operate through extensive earlier periods, we discussed maintenance levels and reference standards of stimulation (that might involve forms of learning) as contextual factors.

The experimental results cited for both appetitive and nonappetitive stimuli represent only a beginning in the identification of contextual setting conditions. To date, remarkably little formal attention has been devoted by behavioral approaches to the variety of contextual conditions that can determine momentary stimulus efficacy. Empirical questions remain concerning:

1. The identities of the contextual manipulations that can determine stimulus efficacy for behavior;

2. The form of the relationship between each set of manipulations (e.g., deprivation-satiation) and the potency of each stimulus affected;

3. Whether there are contextual operations that can produce comparable effects on stimulus function;

4. Whether such operations affect different stimuli (and their roles) in the same or in different ways;

5. How long-term maintenance patterns can determine the impact of contextual setting operations on the efficacy of a stimulus; and

6. Whether there are changes in the effectiveness of stimuli other than that stimulus for which a contextual setting condition has been specifically implemented.

Answers to such questions about the operation of contextual setting conditions are essential for a more complete understanding of the determinants of behavior, including social behavior.

REFERENCES

Asch, S. *Social psychology.* New York: Prentice-Hall, 1952.

Bacon, W. E., & Stanley, W. C. Effect of deprivation level in puppies on performance maintained by a passive person reinforcer. *Journal of Comparative and Physiological Psychology,* 1963, **56,** 783-785.

Baron, R. M. Social reinforcement effects as a function of social reinforcement history. *Psychological Review,* 1966, **73,** 527-539.

Beach, F. A. Current concepts of play in animals. *American Naturalist,* 1945, **79,** 523-541.

Berkowitz, H., Butterfield, E. C., & Zigler, E. The effectiveness of social reinforcers on persistence and learning tasks following positive and negative social interactions. *Journal of Personality and Social Psychology,* 1965, **2,** 706-714.

Berlyne, D. E. Novelty and curiosity as determinants of exploratory behavior. *British Journal of Psychology,* 1950, **41,** 68-80.

Berlyne, D. E. The arousal and satiation of perceptual curiosity in the rat. Journal of Comparative and Physiological Psychology, 1955, **48,** 238-246.

Berlyne, D. E. Attention to change, conditioned inhibition ($_S I_R$) and stimulus satiation. *British Journal of Psychology,* 1957, **48,** 138-140.

Berlyne, D. E. *Conflict, arousal, and curiosity.* New York: McGraw-Hill, 1960.

Bevan, W. The concept of adaptation in modern psychology. *Journal of Psychology,* 1965, **59,** 73-93.

Bevan, W., & Adamson, R. Reinforcers and reinforcement: Their relation to maze performance. *Journal of Experimental Psychology,* 1960, **59,** 226-232.

Bevan, W., & Adamson, R. Internal referents and the concept of reinforcement. In N. F. Washburne (Ed.), *Decisions, values, and groups.* Vol. 2. New York: Pergamon Press, 1963. Pp. 453-472.

Bijou, S. W., & Baer, D. M. Some methodological contributions from a functional analysis of child development. In L. P. Lipsitt and C. C. Spiker (Eds.), *Advances in child development and behavior.* Vol. 1. New York: Academic Press, 1963. Pp. 197-231.

Black, R. W. Shifts in magnitude of reward and contrast effects in instrumental and selective learning: A reinterpretation. *Psychological Review,* 1968, **75,** 114-126.

Brethower, D. M., & Reynolds, G. S. A facilitative effect of punishment on unpunished behavior. *Journal of the Experimental Analysis of Behavior,* 1962, **5,** 191-199.

Brogden, W. J., Lipman, E. A., & Culler, E. The role of incentive in conditioning and extinction. *American Journal of Psychology,* 1938, **51,** 109-117.

Bullock, D. H., & Smith, W. C. An effect of repeated conditioning-extinction upon operant strength. *Journal of Experimental Psychology,* 1953, **46,** 349-352.

Butler, R. A. The effect of deprivation of visual incentives on visual exploration in monkeys. *Journal of Comparative and Physiological Psychology,* 1957, **50,** 177-179.

Cantor, G. N. Children's "like-dislike" ratings of familiarized and nonfamiliarized visual stimuli. *Journal of Experimental Child Psychology,* 1968, **6,** 651-657.

Cantor, G. N., & Cantor, J. H. Discriminative reaction time performance in preschool children as related to stimulus familiarization. *Journal of Experimental Child Psychology,* 1965, **2,** 1-9.

Cantor, J. H., & Cantor, G. N. Observing behavior in children as a function of stimulus novelty. *Child Development,* 1964, **35,** 119-128.

Cantor, J. H., & Cantor, G. N. Functions relating children's observing behavior to amount and recency of stimulus familiarization. *Journal of Experimental Child Psychology,* 1966, **72,** 859-863.

Clark, R. D., & Willems, E. P. Where is the risky shift? Dependence on instructions. *Journal of Personality and Social Psychology,* 1969, **13,** 215-221.

Cook, H., & Vachon, J. Satiation of a verbal cue in problem solving in French speaking children. *Psychonomic Science,* 1968, **11,** 208.

Crandall, V. C., Good, S., & Crandall, V. J. The reinforcement effects of adult reactions and nonreactions on children's achievement expectations: A replication study. *Child Development,* 1964, **35,** 485-497.

Dember, W. N., & Earl, R. W. Analysis of exploratory, manipulatory, and curiosity behaviors. *Psychological Review,* 1957, **64,** 91-96.

Dorwart, W., Ezerman, R., Lewis, M., & Rosenhan, D. The effects of brief social deprivation on social and nonsocial reinforcement. *Journal of Personality and Social Psychology,* 1965, **2,** 111-115.

Dufort, R. H., Guttman, N., & Kimble, G. A. One-trial discrimination reversal in the white rat. *Journal of Comparative and Physiological Psychology,* 1954, **47,** 248-249.

Dulsky, S. G. The effect of a change of background on recall and relearning. *Journal of Experimental Psychology,* 1935, **18,** 725-740.

Dunham, P. J. Contrasted conditions of reinforcement: A selective critique. *Psychological Bulletin,* 1968, **69,** 295-315.

Eisenberger, R. Is there a deprivation-satiation function for social approval? *Psychological Bulletin,* 1970, **74,** 255-275.

Endo, G. T. Social drive or arousal: A test of two theories of social isolation. *Journal of Experimental Child Psychology,* 1968, **6,** 61-74.

Endsley, R. C. Effects of differential prior exposure on preschool children's subsequent choice of novel stimuli. *Psychonomic Science,* 1967, 7, 411-412.

Erickson, M. T. Effects of social deprivation and satiation on verbal conditioning in children. *Journal of Comparative and Physiological Psychology,* 1962, **55,** 953-957.

Fagan, J. F. & Witryol, S. L. The effects of instructional set and delay of reward on children's learning in a simultaneous discrimination task. *Child Development,* 1966, **37,** 433-438.

Fox, S. S. Self-maintained sensory input and sensory deprivation in monkeys: A behavioral and neuropharmacological study. *Journal of Comparative and Physiological Psychology,* 1962, **55,** 438-444.

Gallimore, R., Tharp, R. G., & Kemp, B. Positive reinforcing function of "negative attention." *Journal of Experimental Child Psychology,* 1969, 8, 140-146.

Gellert, E. The effects of changes in group composition on the dominant behaviour of young children. *British Journal of Social and Clinical Psychology,* 1962, **1,** 168-181.

Gewirtz, J. L. Three determinants of attention-seeking in young children. *Monographs of the Society for Research in Child Development,* 1954, **19**(2, Whole No. 59).

Gewirtz, J. L. A learning analysis of the effects of normal stimulation, privation and deprivation on the acquisition of social motivation and attachment. In B. M. Foss (Ed.), *Determinants of infant behaviour.* London: Methuen (New York: Wiley), 1961. Pp. 213-299.

Gewirtz, J. L. Deprivation and satiation of social stimuli as determinants of their reinforcing efficacy. In J. P. Hill (Ed.), *Minnesota symposia on child psychology.* Vol. 1. Minneapolis: Univ. of Minnesota Press, 1967. Pp. 3-56.

Gewirtz, J. L. On designing the functional environment of the child to facilitate behavioral development. In L. L. Dittmann (Ed.), *Early child care: The new perspectives.* New York: Atherton Press, 1968. Pp. 169-213.(a)

Gewirtz, J. L. The role of stimulation in models for child development. In L. L. Dittmann (Ed.), *Early child care: The new perspectives.* New York: Atherton Press, 1968. Pp. 139-168.(b)

Gewirtz, J. L. Mechanisms of social learning: Some roles of stimulation and behavior in early human development. In D. A. Goslin (Ed.), *Handbook of socialization theory and research.* Chicago: Rand McNally, 1969. Pp. 57-212.(a)

Gewirtz, J. L. Potency of a social reinforcer as a function of satiation and recovery. *Developmental Psychology,* 1969, **1,** 2-13.(b)

Gewirtz, J. L. Conditional responding as a model for observational, imitative learning and vicarious-reinforcement. In H. W. Reese (Ed.), *Advances in child development and behavior.* Vol. 6. New York: Academic Press, 1971. Pp. 273-304.(a)

Gewirtz, J. L. The roles of overt responding and extrinsic reinforcement in "self-" and "vicarious-reinforcement" phenomena and in "observational learning" and imitation. In R. Glaser (Ed.), *The nature of reinforcement.* New York: Academic Press, 1971. Pp. 279-309.(b)

Gewirtz, J. L. Stimulation, learning, and motivation principles for day-care settings. In E. H. Grotberg (Ed.), *Day care: Resources for decisions*. Washington: U.S. Office of Economic Opportunity (Pamphlet 6106-1). June 1971. Pp. 173-226.(c)

Gewirtz, J. L. Deficiency conditions of stimulation and the reversal of their effects via enrichment. In Monks, F. J., Hartup, W. W., & de Wit, J. (Eds.), *Determinants of behavioral development*. London & New York: Academic Press, 1972.

Gewirtz, J. L., & Baer, D. M. Deprivation and satiation of social reinforcers as drive conditions. *Journal of Abnormal and Social Psychology*, 1958, **57**, 165-172.(a)

Gewirtz, J. L., & Baer, D. M. The effect of brief social deprivation on behaviors for a social reinforcer. *Journal of Abnormal and Social Psychology*, 1958, **56**, 49-56.(b)

Gewirtz, J. L., Baer, D. M., & Roth, C. H. A note on the similar effects of low social availability of an adult and brief social deprivation on young children's behavior. *Child Development*, 1958, **29**, 149-152.

Gewirtz, J. L., Jones, L. V., & Waerneryd, K. E. Stimulus units and range of experienced stimuli as determinants of generalization-discrimination gradients. *Journal of Experimental Psychology*, 1956, **51**, 51-57.

Glanzer, M. Stimulus satiation: An explanation of spontaneous alternation and related phenomena. *Psychological Review*, 1953, **60**, 257-268.

Glanzer, M. Curiosity, exploratory drive, and stimulus satiation. *Psychological Bulletin*, 1958, **55**, 302-315.

Gullickson, G. R. A note on children's selection of novel auditory stimuli. *Journal of Experimental Child Psychology*, 1966, **4**, 158-162.

Harlow, H. F. Learning set and error factor theory. In S. Koch (Ed.), *Psychology: A study of a science*. Vol. 2. New York: McGraw-Hill, 1959. Pp. 492-537.

Harris, L. The effects of relative novelty on children's choice behavior. *Journal of Experimental Child Psychology*, 1965, **2**, 297-305.

Hartup, W. W. Nurturance and nurturance-withdrawal in relation to the dependency behavior of young children. *Child Development*, 1958, **29**, 191-201.

Hartup, W. W. Friendship status and the effectiveness of peers as reinforcing agents. *Journal of Experimental Child Psychology*, 1964, **1**, 154-162.

Hartup, W. W., & Himeno, Y. Social isolation versus interaction with adults in relation to aggression in preschool children. *Journal of Abnormal and Social Psychology*, 1959, **59**, 17-22.

Hebb, D. O. On the nature of fear. *Psychological Review*, 1946, **53**, 259-276.

Hebb, D. O. *The organization of behavior*. New York: Wiley, 1949.

Hebb, D. O. *A textbook of psychology*. Philadelphia: Saunders, 1966.

Helson, H. Adaptation-level as frame of reference for prediction of psychophysical data. *American Journal of Psychology*, 1947, **60**, 1-29.

Helson, H. Adaptation-level as a basis for a quantitative theory of frames of reference. *Psychological Review*, 1948, **55**, 297-313.

Helson, H. Adaptation-level theory. In S. Koch (Ed.), *Psychology: A study of a science,* Vol. 1. *Sensory, perceptual, and physiological foundations.* New York: McGraw-Hill, 1959. Pp. 565-621.

Helson, H. *Adaptation-level theory* New York: Harper, 1964.

Helson, H., & Avant, L. L. Stimulus generalization as a function of contextual stimuli. *Journal of Experimental Psychology,* 1967, 73, 565-567.

Herrnstein, R. J., & Brady, J. V. Interactions among components of a multiple schedule. *Journal of the Experimental Analysis of Behavior,* 1958, 1, 293-301.

Hilgard, E. R., & Humphreys, L. G. The effect of supporting and antagonistic voluntary instructions on conditioned discrimination. *Journal of Experimental Psychology,* 1938, 22, 291-304.

Hill, K. T., & Stevenson, H. W. Effectiveness of social reinforcement following social and sensory deprivation. *Journal of Abnormal and Social Psychology,* 1964, 68, 579-584.

Hinde, R. A. Factors governing the changes in strength of a partially inborn response, as shown by the mobbing behaviour of the Chaffinch (*Fringilla coelebs*): II. The waning of the response. *Proceedings of the Royal Society,* Ser. B, 1954, 142B, 331-358.

Hinde, R. A. Factors governing the changes in strength of a partially inborn response, as shown by the mobbing behaviour of the Chaffinch (*Fringilla coelebs*): III. The interaction of short-term and long-term incremental and decremental effects. *Proceedings of the Royal Society,* Ser. B, 1960, 153, 398-420.

Jones, A. Supplementary report: Information deprivation and irrelevant drive as determiners of an instrumental response. *Journal of Experimental Psychology,* 1961, 62, 310-311.

Jones, A. Drive and incentive variables associated with the statistical properties of sequences of stimuli. *Journal of Experimental Psychology,* 1964, 67, 423-431.

Jones, A., Wilkinson, H. J., & Braden, I. Information deprivation as a motivational variable. *Journal of Experimental Psychology,* 1961, 62, 126-137.

Kantor, J. R. *Interbehavioral psychology.* Bloomington, Ind.: Principia Press, 1959.

Kimble, G. A. *Hilgard and Marquis' conditioning and learning.* New York: Appleton-Century-Crofts, 1961.

Kish, G. B. Studies of sensory reinforcement. In W. K. Honig (Ed.), *Operant behavior: Areas of research and application.* New York: Appleton-Century-Crofts, 1966. Pp. 109-159.

Kozma, A. The effects of anxiety, stimulation, and isolation on social reinforcer effectiveness. *Journal of Experimental Child Psychology,* 1969, 8, 1-8.

Landau, R., & Gewirtz, J. L. Differential satiation for a social reinforcing stimulus as a determinant of its efficacy in conditioning. *Journal of Experimental Child Psychology,* 1967, 5, 391-405.

Lewis, M. Social isolation: A parametric study of its effect on social reinforcement. *Journal of Experimental Child Psychology,* 1965, 2, 205-218.

Lewis, M., & Goldberg, S. The acquisition and violation of expectancy: An experimental paradigm. *Journal of Experimental Child Psychology,* 1969, 7, 70-80.

Lewis, M., & Richman, S. Social encounters and their effects on subsequent reinforcement. *Journal of Abnormal and Social Psychology,* 1964, 69, 253-257.

Lockard, R. B. Some effects of maintenance luminance and strain differences upon the self-exposure to light by rats. *Journal of Comparative and Physiological Psychology,* 1962, **55,** 1118-1123.

Lockard, R. B. A method of analysis and classification of repetitive response systems. *Psychological Review,* 1964, **71,** 141-147.

Maltzman, I. Theoretical conceptions of semantic conditioning and generalization. In T. Dixon & D. Horton (Eds.), *Verbal behavior and general behavior theory.* New York: Prentice-Hall, 1968.

McArthur, L. A., & Zigler, E. Level of satiation on social reinforcers and valence of the reinforcing agent as determinants of social reinforcer effectiveness. *Developmental Psychology,* 1969, **1,** 739-746.

McCall, R. B., & Kagan, J. Stimulus-schema discrepancy and attention in the infant. *Journal of Experimental Child Psychology,* 1967, **5,** 381-390.

McClelland, D. C., Atkinson, J. W., Clark, R. A., & Lowell, E. L. *The achievement motive.* New York: Appleton-Century-Crofts, 1953.

McCoy, N., & Zigler, E. Social reinforcer effectiveness as a function of the relationship between child and adult. *Journal of Personality and Social Psychology,* 1965, **1,** 604-612.

Mendel, G. Children's preferences for differing degrees of novelty. *Child Development,* 1965, **36,** 453-465.

Montgomery, K. C. Exploratory behavior as a function of "similarity" of stimulus situations. *Journal of Comparative and Physiological Psychology,* 1953, **46,** 129-133.

Odom, R. D. Effects of auditory and visual stimulus deprivation and satiation on children's performance in an operant task. *Journal of Experimental Child Psychology,* 1964, **1,** 16-25.

Parke, R. D. Nurturance, nurturance withdrawal, and resistance to deviation. *Child Development,* 1967, **38,** 1101-1110.

Parke, R. D., & Walters, R. H. Some factors influencing the efficacy of punishment training for inducing response inhibition. *Monographs of the Society for Research in Child Development.* 1967, **32** (Whole No. 109).

Patterson, G. R. Behavioral techniques based upon social learning: An additional base for developing behavior modification technologies. In C. M. Franks (Ed.), *Behavior therapy: Appraisal and status.* New York: McGraw-Hill, 1969. Pp. 341-374.

Patterson, G. R., Littman, R., & Hinsey, W. C. Parental effectiveness as reinforcers in the laboratory and its relation to child rearing practices and child adjustment in the classroom. *Journal of Personality,* 1964, **32,** 180-199.

Premack, D. Toward empirical behavior laws: I. Positive reinforcement. *Psychological Review,* 1959, **66,** 219-233.

Premack, D. Reversibility of the reinforcement relation. *Science,* 1962, **136,** 255-257.

Premack, D. On some boundary conditions of contrast. In J. T. Tapp (Ed.), *Reinforcement and behavior.* New York: Academic Press, 1969. Pp. 120-145.

Premack, D., & Collier, G. Analysis of nonreinforcement variables affecting response probability. *Psychological Monographs,* 1962, **76**(5, Whole No. 524).

Reynolds, G. S. An analysis of interactions in a multiple schedule. *Journal of the Experimental Analysis of Behavior,* 1961, **4,** 107-117.(a)

Reynolds, G. S. Behavioral contrast. *Journal of the Experimental Analysis of Behavior,* 1961, **4,** 57-71.(b)

Rosenhan, D. Aloneness and togetherness as drive conditions in children. *Journal of Experimental Research in Personality,* 1967, **2,** 32-40.

Sokolov, E. N. *Perception and the conditioned reflex.* New York: Macmillan, 1963.

Stevens, S. S. Adaptation-level vs. the relativity of judgment. *American Journal of Psychology,* 1958, **71,** 633-646.

Stevenson, H. W., & Odom, R. D. Effects of pretraining on the reinforcing value of visual stimuli. *Child Development,* 1961, **32,** 739-744.

Stevenson, H. W., & Odom, R. D. The effectiveness of social reinforcement following two conditions of social deprivation. *Journal of Abnormal and Social Psychology,* 1962, **65,** 429-431.

Stevenson, H. W., & Hill, K. T. The effects of social reinforcement and nonreinforcement following success and failure. *Journal of Personality,* 1965, **33,** 418-427.

Stone, L. J., & Hokanson, J. E. Arousal reduction via self-punitive behavior. *Journal of Personality and Social Psychology,* 1969, **12,** 72-79.

Terrace, H. S. Behavioral contrast and the peak shift: Effects of extended discrimination training. *Journal of the Experimental Analysis of Behavior,* 1966, **9,** 613-617.

Tiktin, S., & Hartup, W. W. Sociometric status and the reinforcing effectiveness of children's peers. *Journal of Experimental Child Psychology,* 1965, **2,** 306-315.

Walters, R. H., & Parke, R. D. Emotional arousal, isolation and discrimination learning in children. *Journal of Experimental Child Psychology,* 1964, **1,** 163-173.

Walters, R. H., & Ray, E. Anxiety, social isolation, and reinforcer effectiveness. *Journal of Personality,* 1960, **28,** 358-367.

Walters, R. H., & Quinn, M. J. The effects of social and sensory deprivation on autokinetic judgments. *Journal of Personality,* 1960, **28,** 210-219.

Weiner, H. Conditioning history and the control of human avoidance and escape responding. *Journal of the Experimental Analysis of Behavior,* 1969, **12,** 1039-1043.(a)

Weiner, H. Controlling human fixed-interval performance. *Journal of the Experimental Analysis of Behavior,* 1969, **12,** 349-373.(b)

Weisberg, P. Effects of reinforcement history on timing (DRL) performance in young children. *Journal of Experimental Child Psychology,* 1970, **9,** 348-362.

Weisman, R., & Premack, D. Punishment and reinforcement produced by reversal of the probability relation between two responses. *Program of the Seventh Annual Scientific Meeting of the Psychonomic Society,* 1966, Pp. 20-21. (Abstract)

Weiss, W., & Margolius, G. The effect of context stimuli on learning and retention. *Journal of Experimental Psychology,* 1954, **48,** 318-322.

Welker, W. I. Variability of play and exploratory behavior in chimpanzees. *Journal of Comparative and Physiological Psychology,* 1956, **49,** 181-185.

Wolff, C., & Maltzman, I. Conditioned orienting reflex and amount of preconditioning habituation. *Proceedings, 76th Annual Convention, APA,* 1968, Pp. 129-130.

chapter 3

Modeling Theory: Some Traditions, Trends, and Disputes[1] | *Albert Bandura*

At the time that Richard Walters and I began our research on social learning, the research stock quotations in the psychological abstracts disclosed modeling to be an inconsequential item. It struck us as exceedingly paradoxical that a commodity that is used routinely by everyone for transmitting, modifying, and regulating human behavior, and without which few would survive the hazardous course of socialization, should not have occupied a prominent place on the "big board" of psychological science.

[1] The research reported in this paper was supported by Research Grant M-5162 from the National Institute of Mental Health, United States Public Health Service.

There are several reasons why modeling had, until recent years, been relatively neglected despite its influential role in psychological functioning. It was handicapped from the outset by being christened at infancy as an instinctual propensity. Even after the phenomenon was cleansed of instinctional properties, it nevertheless conveyed the impression that imitation is principally a characteristic of people who are anxious, dependent, conforming, and who are lacking in intelligence, in self-confidence, and in self-esteem. These prosaic correlates may obtain in ambiguous laboratory experiments in which models perform inconsequential responses that have little or no functional value for subjects who are expected to participate in psychological experiments as part of institutional or academic course requirements. In these situations the main rewards for the brighter and bolder subjects are usually derived from outwitting the experimenter. On the other hand, when modeling is purposefully used to teach people how to communicate verbally, how to behave socially, how to drive automobiles, to swim, to perform surgical operations, and to conduct psychological research, the more talented are likely to derive the greater benefits from observation of exemplary models.

Another factor that detracted from the significance of research dealing with modeling phenomena was the widespread use of a restricted experimental paradigm. In these studies, a model performs a specific set of responses, and observers are subsequently tested for precise matching behavior in similar or identical situations. Under these circumscribed conditions, experiments could yield only mimicry of specific modeled responses. This led many researchers to place severe limitations on the behavioral changes that can be attributed to modeling influences.

In an attempt to demonstrate that the limitations ascribed to modeling were inherent in the experimental methodology rather than in the phenomenon itself, we conducted several experiments requiring a higher-order form of modeling (Bandura & Harris, 1966; Bandura & McDonald, 1963; Bandura & Mischel, 1965). These studies used a paradigm in which persons display a consistent style of behavior to diverse stimuli, and tests for generalized modeling effects are subsequently conducted by different experimenters, in different social settings with the models absent, and with different stimulus items. The results disclose that observers respond to new stimulus situations in a manner consistent with the models' dispositions even though subjects had never observed the models responding to these particular stimuli.

In this higher-order form of modeling, the performer's behavior conveys information to observers about the characteristics of appropriate responses. Observers must abstract common attributes exemplified in diverse modeled responses and formulate a principle for generating similar patterns of behavior. Responses performed by subjects that embody the observationally derived rule are likely to resemble the behavior that the model would be inclined to exhibit under similar circumstances, even though subjects had never witnessed the model's behavior in these new situations. In social learning theory matching phenomena are designated as "modeling." This term was adopted because modeling influences have much broader psychological effects than the simple response mimicry implied by the term "imitation."

The complex changes that modeling influences can produce are further revealed in experimental paradigms using multiple models who display diverse patterns of behavior (Bandura, Ross, & Ross, 1963). In subsequent tests, observers generally exhibit relatively novel responses representing amalgams of elements from the different models. Moreover, the specific admixtures of behavioral elements vary from subject to subject. If these persons were now to serve as models for other observers, one would expect additional behavioral innovation and a gradual imitative evolution of novel patterns of behavior that might bear little resemblance to those exhibited by the original models. Depending on how they are used, modeling influences can thus produce not only specific mimicry but also generative and innovative behavior.

The discussion so far has shown that modeling influences effect broader and more complex psychological changes than is commonly assumed. With few exceptions, the experiments conducted in our laboratory use a nonresponse acquisition procedure in which a person simply observes a model's behavior, but otherwise exhibits no overt responses, nor is administered any reinforcing stimuli during the acquisition period. Since, in this mode of response acquisition, observers can learn the modeled responses only in representational forms, the modeling paradigm provides an interesting means of studying symbolic processes and their performance guiding functions.

The recent years have witnessed a rapid growth of research and theorizing about modeling phenomena. Indeed, for a while, it looked as though the number of theoretical analyses of imitation would exceed the number of well-designed empirical studies. Most of the current research in this area is being conducted either from the operant conditioning perspective or within the social learning framework. Both of these approaches make similar assumptions about the factors regulating preexisting matching responses, but they differ markedly on the conditions governing the acquisition of response patterns through observation.

OPERANT CONDITIONING ANALYSIS

The operant conditioning analysis of modeling (Baer & Sherman, 1964; Baer, Peterson, & Sherman, 1967) relies entirely upon the standard three-component paradigm $S^d \rightarrow R \rightarrow S^r$, where S^d denotes the modeled stimulus, R represents an overt matching response, and S^r designates the reinforcing stimulus. Observational learning is presumably achieved through a process of differential reinforcement. When imitative behavior has been positively reinforced and divergent responses either nonrewarded or punished, the behavior of others comes to function as discriminative stimuli for matching responses.

In everyday life and in most laboratory studies of delayed imitation, modeled behavior is often reproduced by observers in the absence of immediate external reinforcement. Consequently, theories postulating that some form of reinforcement is necessary for learning must identify an alternative source of reinforcement. In the formulation advanced by Baer it is assumed that if accurate reproduction of modeling stimuli is consistently rewarded, behavioral similarity per se acquires secondary reinforcing properties. After similarity has become reinforcing in its own right, people are disposed toward performing imitative responses which are strengthened and maintained by their endowed reward value. This issue will be discussed later in greater detail.

It is difficult to see how the operant analysis is applicable to observational learning in which an observer does not overtly perform the model's responses during the acquisition phase, reinforcers are not administered either to the model or to the observer, and the acquired response may be performed for the first time days or weeks later in situations in which the model is no longer present. In the latter case, which represents one of the most prevalent forms of social learning, two of the events, namely the matching response and the reinforcing stimulus ($R \rightarrow S^r$) in the three-term paradigm, are absent during acquisition, and the third element, the modeling stimulus (S^d) is typically absent from the situation in which the observationally learned response is performed.

In a recent operant conditioning analysis of imitation, Gewirtz (1969) conceptualizes modeling as being analogous to the matching-to-sample paradigm used to study discrimination learning. In this procedure, a subject chooses from among a number of comparison stimuli one that shares a common property with the sample stimulus. Although modeling and matching-to-sample performances have some likeness in that both involve a matching process, they can hardly be equated. A person can achieve errorless choices in matching comparison operatic arias with a sample Wagnerian recital, but still remain totally unable to perform the vocal behavior contained in the sample. Accurate stimulus discrimination is a precondition for, but not equivalent with, observational response learning.

Observational learning is primarily concerned with processes whereby observers organize response elements into new patterns of behavior at a symbolic level on the basis of information conveyed by modeling stimuli. The major controversy among theories of observational learning centers around the basic question of whether new responses are learned and integrated centrally or whether they are organized peripherally during overt performance. Fortunately, it is possible to obtain an index of response learning independent of performance simply by asking subjects to describe the behavior that they have observed. Evidence that observers can describe accurately complex patterns and sequences of responses as a result of exposure to modeling stimuli prior to behavioral reproduction or to appearance of reinforcing events argues for a central response integrative mechanism. Designating observational learning as "generalized imitation" (Gewirtz, 1969) in no way explains the phenomenon; it essentially represents descriptive labeling in the guise of explanation. Later we will show that a formulation that contends that people imitate because they have been occasionally reinforced for imitation does not have much predictive power.

Like the earlier theory of imitation developed by Miller and Dollard (1941), the operant conditioning interpretation of modeling phenomena accounts satisfactorily for the control of previously learned matching responses by their stimulus antecedents and their immediate consequences. However, it fails to explain how a new matching response is acquired observationally in the first place.

Another closely related issue is concerned with whether reinforcement is a prerequisite for observational learning. This question can be most definitively resolved by the use of infrahuman subjects whose reinforcement history is fully controlled. In a preliminary study, Foss (1964) found that birds will imitate unusual sound patterns played on a tape recorder in the absence of any prior reinforcement of matching responses. We should note here that the controversy among theories of observational learning is primarily concerned with the manner in which reinforcement affects learning rather than with whether reinforcement plays a role in the acquisition process. Under conditions in which either models or observers themselves are repeatedly reinforced as they perform an ongoing series of responses, observation of reinforcing outcomes occurring early in the sequence might be expected to increase the observer's vigilance in respect to subsequently modeled behavior. The anticipation of positive reinforcement for reproducing matching responses by the observer may, therefore, indirectly influence the course of observational learning by enhancing and focusing observing responses. Anticipated consequences can affect other cognitive activities that partly determine response acquisition and retention.

SOCIAL LEARNING ANALYSIS

When a person observes a model's behavior without simultaneously performing the responses, he can acquire the modeled responses while they are occurring only in representational forms. The social learning analysis of observational learning (Bandura, 1969a; 1971b) assumes that modeling influences operate principally through their informative function, and that observers acquire mainly symbolic representations of modeled events rather than specific stimulus-response associations. Modeling phenomena, in fact, involve four interrelated subprocesses, each with its own set of controlling variables. A comprehensive theory of observational learning must therefore encompass the diverse subsystems governing the broader phenomena.

ATTENTIONAL PROCESSES

One of the main component functions in observational learning involves attentional processes. Simply exposing persons to sequences of modeling stimuli does not in itself guarantee that they will attend closely to the cues, that they will necessarily select from the total stimulus complex the most relevant events, or that they will even perceive accurately the cues to which their attention has been directed. An observer will fail to acquire matching behavior, at the sensory registration level, if he does not attend to, recognize, or differentiate the distinctive features of the model's responses. Stimulus contiguity must, therefore, be accompanied by discriminative observation to produce learning.

A number of attention controlling variables, some related to incentive conditions, others to observer characteristics, and still others to the properties of the modeling cues themselves, will be influential in determining which modeling stimuli will be observed and which will be ignored.

RETENTION PROCESSES

Another basic component function involved in observational learning, but one that has virtually been ignored in theories of imitation, concerns the retention of modeled events. In order to reproduce social behavior without the continued presence of external modeling cues, a person must retain the original observational inputs in some symbolic form. This is a particularly interesting problem in instances in which persons acquire social patterns of behavior observationally, and retain them over extended periods, even though the response tendencies are rarely, if ever, activated into overt performance until attainment of age or social status at which the activity is appropriate and permissible.

Among the many variables governing retention processes, *rehearsal operations* effectively stabilize and strengthen acquired responses (Bandura & Jeffery, 1971; Michael & Maccoby, 1961). The level of observational learning can, therefore, be considerably enhanced through practice or covert rehearsal of modeled response sequences, particularly if the rehearsal is interposed after natural segments of a larger modeled pattern. Of greater import is evidence that covert rehearsal, which can readily be engaged in when overt performance is either impeded or impracticable, may likewise enhance retention of acquired matching responses.

Symbolic coding of modeling stimuli is even more efficacious than rehearsal in facilitating long-term retention of matching behavior (Bandura

& Jeffery, 1971). During exposure to stimulus sequences, observers tend to code, to classify, and to reorganize elements into familiar and more easily remembered schemes. Observational learning involves two representational systems—an imaginal and a verbal one. After modeling stimuli have been coded into images or words for memory representation, they function as guides for subsequent response retrieval and reproduction.

Imagery formation is assumed to occur through a process of sensory conditioning. That is, during the period of exposure, modeling stimuli elicit in observers perceptual responses that become sequentially associated and centrally integrated on the basis of contiguity. Under conditions in which stimulus events are highly correlated, as when a name is consistently associated with a given person, it is virtually impossible to hear the name without experiencing imagery of the person's physical characteristics. Research findings indicate that, in the course of observation, transitory perceptual phenomena produce relatively enduring, retrievable images of modeled sequences of behavior. Later, reinstatement of imaginal mediators serves as a guide for reproduction of matching responses.

The second representational system, which probably accounts for the notable speed of observational learning and long-term retention of modeled contents by humans, involves verbal coding of observed events. Most of the cognitive processes that regulate behavior are primarily verbal rather than visual. To take a simple example, the route traversed by a model can be acquired, retained, and later reproduced more accurately by verbal coding of the visual information into a sequence of right–left turns (e.g., RRLRR) than by reliance upon visual imagery of the itinerary. Observational learning and retention are facilitated by such codes because they can carry a great deal of information in an easily stored form. After modeled responses have been transformed into readily usable verbal symbols, performances of matching behavior on later occasions can effectively be controlled by covert self-directions.

The influential role of symbolic representation in observational learning is disclosed by a study (Bandura, Grusec, & Menlove, 1966) in which children were exposed to several complex sequences of behavior modeled on film. During exposure the children watched attentively, coded the novel responses into their verbal equivalents as they were performed by the model, or counted rapidly while watching the film to prevent implicit verbal coding of modeling stimuli. A subsequent test of observational learning disclosed that children who verbally coded the modeled patterns reproduced significantly more matching responses than those in the viewing-alone condition who, in turn, showed a higher level of acquisition than children who engaged in competing symbolization.

Further supporting evidence for the influence of symbolic coding operations in the acquisition and retention of modeled responses is furnished by Gerst (1971) in a recently completed dissertation at Stanford. College students observed a filmed model perform complex motor responses composed of movements taken from the alphabet of the deaf. Immediately after observing each modeled response, subjects engaged in one of four symbolic activities for a period of 1 minute. One group reinstated the response through vivid imagery; a second group coded the modeling stimuli into concrete verbal terms by describing the specific response elements and their movements; the third group generated concise labels that incorporated the essential ingredients of the responses. For example, a pretzel-shaped response might be labeled as an orchestra conductor moving his baton in an orchestral finale. Subjects assigned to the control group performed mental calculations to impede symbolic coding of the modeling stimuli.

Subjects reproduced the modeled responses immediately after the coding session, and following a 15-minute period during which they performed a distracting task designed to prevent symbolic rehearsal of modeled responses.

In Figure 1 the percentage of modeled behavior correctly reproduced is plotted as a function of symbolic coding and temporal factors. Compared to the performance of control subjects who had no opportunity to generate symbolic mediators, all three coding operations enhanced observational learning. Concise labeling and imaginal codes were equally effective in aiding immediate reproduction of modeled responses and both systems proved superior in this respect to the concrete verbal form.

The delayed test for retention of matching responses showed concise labeling to be the best coding system for memory representation. Subjects in this condition retained significantly more matching responses than those who relied upon imagery and concrete verbalizations. Subjects in all groups showed a loss of modeled responses over time. The decrement is most likely attributable to the fact that the responses were exceedingly complex, that they were formed by different combinations of a common set of behavioral elements that would produce considerable associative

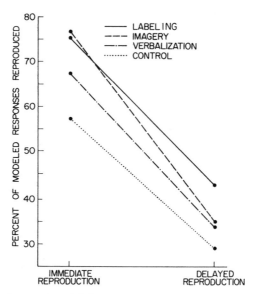

FIG. 1. Percent of modeled responses reproduced by control subjects and those who coded the modeled behavior as either images, concrete verbal descriptions, or summary labels for memory representation (Gerst, 1971).

interference, and that subjects had no opportunity to rehearse the responses either symbolically or overtly.

The relative superiority of the summary labeling code is shown even more clearly when matching performances are scored according to a stringent criterion requiring all the response elements to be reproduced in the exact sequence in which they were originally modeled. Subjects who coded the modeling stimuli into concise labels were able to reproduce approximately twice as many well-integrated responses in the retention test as compared to matching performances of the other groups. Moreover, modeled responses for which subjects retained the summary codes were reproduced at a higher level of accuracy (52%) than those for which the code was lost (7%).

A study by Bandura and Jeffery (1971) further demonstrates that observational learning is better understood in terms of information processing than in terms of overt enactment of responses. Adults observed a model perform complex movement configurations. Noncoders were left to their own devices in learning the modeled performances. Coders, on the other hand, learned each modeled activity by dividing it into its component parts, assigning letter or number associates to each component, and storing the entire pattern in memory as an ensemble letter or numerical code. The modeled behavior was later reconstructed from the reductive code by translating sequentially each of the code elements into its corresponding action.

Memory codes are of little value if they are forgotten, as the study by Gerst (1971) shows. The present experiment examined the retention enhancing effects of different forms of rehearsal. Immediately after the test for observational learning, subjects in each condition overtly performed the modeled responses, rehearsed the symbolic codes embodying the responses, or were provided with no opportunities to practice what they had seen. In a subsequent delayed test of response reproduction, subjects performed all the modeled configurations to the best of their recollection.

Figure 2 shows the percent of modeled responses accurately reproduced as a function of symbolic coding, rehearsal, and retention interval. Consistent with previous findings, observational learning is improved by symbolic coding of modeled activities. Retention of observationally learned responses is substantially aided by symbolic coding, by rehearsal, and by the interactive effects of these two factors. The interaction indicates that rehearsal in any form does not improve retention in subjects who failed to code the modeled performances for storage and retrieval. Coders, on the other hand, benefited significantly from symbolic rehearsal but not from repeated enactment of the responses. Indeed, the highest matching performances were attained by subjects who transformed the model's behavior into symbols and rehearsed the symbolic code from which the motor responses could easily be reconstructed.

Gewirtz (1969) questions the value of theories of modeling that include symbolic processes on the grounds that the symbolic events are inferred from the behavior they are designed to explain. This criticism may apply to theories that attribute behavior to hypothetical internal agencies having only a tenuous relationship to antecedent events and to the behavior that they supposedly explain. We should emphasize here that in the aforementioned experiments, symbolic events are independently manipulated rather than inferred from matching responses.

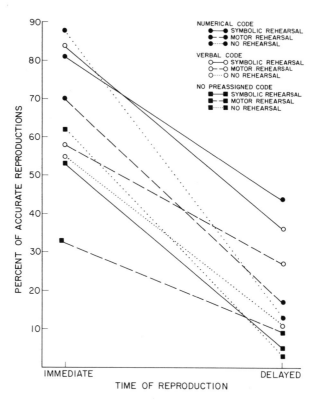

FIG. 2. Percent of modeled performances accurately reproduced as a function of symbolic coding, rehearsal and retention interval.

MOTOR REPRODUCTION PROCESSES

The third major component of modeling phenomena is concerned with motor reproduction processes. This involves the use of symbolic representations of modeled patterns to guide overt performances. The process of representational guidance is essentially the same as that of response learning under conditions in which a person behaviorally follows an externally depicted pattern, or is directed through a series of instructions to enact novel response sequences. The only difference is that in the latter cases, performance is directed by external cues, whereas in delayed modeling, behavioral reproduction is monitored by symbolic counterparts of absent stimuli.

The rate and level of observational learning will be governed partly, at the motoric level, by the availability of necessary component responses. Complex behavior patterns are produced by combinations of previously learned components which may, in themselves, represent relatively intricate compounds. In instances in which observers lack some of the necessary components, the constituent elements can best be established through reinforced modeling and then, in a stepwise fashion, increasingly complex compounds can be acquired imitatively.

In many instances modeled response patterns have been acquired and retained in representational forms, but they cannot be reproduced behaviorally because of physical limitations. Few basketball enthusiasts could ever successfully match the remarkable performances of a towering professional player regardless of their vigilance and dutiful rehearsal.

Accurate behavioral enactment of modeling cues is also difficult to achieve under conditions in which the model's performance is governed by subtle adjustment of internal responses that are unobservable and not easily communicable. An aspiring operatic singer may benefit considerably from observing an accomplished voice instructor; nevertheless, skilled vocal reproduction is hampered by the fact that the model's laryngeal and respiratory muscular responses are neither readily observable nor easily described verbally.

The problem of behavioral reproduction is further complicated in the case of highly coordinated motor skills, such as golf, in which a person cannot observe many of the responses he is making, and must therefore primarily rely on proprioceptive feedback cues and verbal reports of onlookers. For these reasons, performances that contain many motor components usually require, in addition to the guidance of a proficient model, varying amounts of overt practice.

MOTIVATIONAL AND REINFORCEMENT PROCESSES

The final component function concerns motivational and reinforcement processes. A person may acquire, retain, and possess the capabilities for skillful execution of modeled behavior, but the learning may rarely be activated into overt performance if negative sanctions or unfavorable incentive conditions obtain. Under such circumstances, when positive incentives are introduced, observational learning is promptly translated into action (Bandura, 1965). Reinforcement variables not only regulate the overt expression of matching behavior but can also affect observational learning by exerting selective control over the types of modeling cues to which a person is most likely to attend. Moreover, they can facilitate selective retention by activating deliberate coding and rehearsal of modeled responses that have high utilitarian value.

Traditional reinforcement approaches have focused their attention almost exclusively on the control of responses through externally administered consequences. According to social learning theory, behavior is maintained not only by directly experienced consequences arising from external sources but also by vicarious reinforcement and by self-reinforcement (Bandura, 1971a). In everyday life, people continually observe the actions of others and the occasions on which they are rewarded, ignored, or punished. Observed consequences not only play an influential role in regulating behavior but also provide a reference standard that determines whether a particular reinforcer that is externally dispensed will function as a reward or as a punishment. Since both direct and vicarious reinforcement inevitably occur together under natural conditions, the interactive effects of these two sources of influence on human behavior are of much greater significance than their independent controlling power.

Most human behavior, of course, is not controlled by immediate external reinforcement. Rather, people regulate their own actions to some extent by self-generated anticipatory and self-evaluative consequences. At this higher level of psychological functioning people set themselves certain performance standards, and they respond to their own behavior in self-rewarding or self-punishing ways, depending on whether their performances fall short of, match, or exceed their self-imposed demands. After a self-monitored reinforcement system has been established, a given performance produces two sets of consequences—a self-evaluative reaction as well as some external ones. In many instances self-generated and externally occurring consequences may conflict, as when certain courses of action are approved and encouraged by others, but if carried out would give rise to self-devaluative reactions. Under these circumstances, the effects of self-reinforcement may prevail over external influences. Conversely, response patterns may be effectively maintained by self-reward under conditions of minimal external support or approval.

FIG. 3. Subprocesses that govern observational learning in the social learning analysis.

If one is interested merely in producing imitative behavior, some of the subprocesses just outlined can be disregarded. An experimenter who repeatedly demonstrates a given set of responses, instructs children to reproduce them, manually prompts the behavior when it fails to occur, and then administers powerful reinforcers, will eventually elicit matching responses in most subjects. It may require 1, 10, or 100 demonstration trials, but if one persists, the desired behavior will eventually be evoked. If, on the other hand, one is interested in identifying the conditions governing modeling phenomena, then a more diverse set of controlling variables must be considered. The critical subprocesses and their determinants are summarized in Figure 3.

Nonmediational theories cannot adequately account for variations in matching performances as a function of symbolic activities (Bandura & Jeffery, 1971; Gerst, 1971), under conditions in which modeling stimuli and reinforcement contingencies remain the same for all subjects. The limitations of conceptual schemes that depict matching responses as controlled solely by external stimuli and reinforcing consequences is also readily apparent in instances when repeated presentation of modeling stimuli under favorable reinforcement conditions fails to produce matching responses. For example, difficulties encountered by Lovaas in producing imitative behavior in some autistic children has stimulated research on attentional deficits (Lovaas, Schriebman, Koegel, & Rehm, 1972). Preliminary findings indicate that autistic children have difficulty in processing information conveyed through different sensory modalities. However, their rate of learning is greatly facilitated by various attention-enhancing procedures (Wasserman, 1968) that could be used effectively in modeling situations. Given evidence that observers often fail to retain what they have learned, nonmediational theories will eventually be forced to consider retention processes, as well.

In any given instance, absence of appropriate matching behavior following exposure to modeling stimuli may result from either failures in sensory registration of modeled events, inadequate coding of modeling stimuli for memory representation, retention decrements, motor deficiencies, or inadequate reinforcement.

THE MODELING PROCESS AND FORM IN WHICH
RESPONSE INFORMATION IS TRANSMITTED

Development of new modes of response, however achieved, requires organization of behavioral elements into certain patterns and sequences.

The process of response integration is markedly facilitated by clear representation of how the various elements must be combined and temporally sequenced. This information can be conveyed through physical demonstration, through pictorial representation, or through verbal description. It can also be inferred from observation of differential consequences accompanying one's trial-and-error performances although, in instances in which the pattern of activity contains a unique combination of elements selected from numerous alternatives, response specification through differential reinforcement is an exceedingly laborious procedure. Luchins and Luchins (1966) report that college students made over a thousand errors and never did fully acquire a complicated sequence of behavior when the only response guidance they received was in the form of differential feedback of correctly performed elements. By contrast, subjects who observed a model demonstrate the required pattern learned the behavior rapidly and were spared the exasperation evidenced by the group guided only by response feedback. Warden and his associates (Warden, Fjeld, & Koch, 1940) likewise found that naive primates who observed the skilled performance of a model achieved instantaneous solutions to intricate problems that had required the primate demonstrators a considerable amount of time to learn on the basis of differential reinforcement of their trial-and-error performances.

We should emphasize here that modeling is primarily concerned with processes whereby representation of patterned activities serves a response guidance function, rather than with the particular form in which response information is presented. A number of conceptual and methodological confusions arise when modeling is defined in terms of how the requisite activities are portrayed. In several experiments, Parton and his associates (Dubanoski & Parton, 1968; Fouts & Parton, 1969) compared the accuracy with which children placed objects in selected locations after observing a film in which object placements were made by hand, by moving the objects with nylon thread, or by a sweep of the camera depicting the objects alone and then in their appropriate locations. As expected, comparable matching performances were obtained regardless of the mode of conveyance.

Human transmitters are used widely in modeling experiments, not because this is the only means of conveying response information, but because under conditions of everyday life, desired response patterns are usually depicted, either deliberately or inadvertently, through social demonstration. Moreover, in most social behavior, the models' actions are the critical events and, therefore, to remove the social model is to erase the behavior. How, for example, can one have a march without a marcher, a verbal response without a vocalizer, or a punch without a puncher?

We might note that in the studies previously cited, the experimental conditions differed mainly in the directness with which models performed the requisite activities. Had children in the group presumably lacking a model been asked how the objects got to their destinations, they would undoubtedly have reported that they were moved by a person rather than by internal propulsion. Investigations of symbolic modeling (Bandura & Mischel, 1965) demonstrate that matching performances can readily be achieved without requiring the physical presence of a model if the essential features of his behavior are accurately depicted either pictorially or verbally. To the extent that live and symbolic modeling convey the same amount of response information and are equally effective in commanding attention, both forms of modeling influences are likely to produce equivalent levels of observational learning.

The phenomenon of verbal modeling, alluded to above, is highly relevant to the issue of instructional control of behavior. In examining the process of verbal control, it is essential to distinguish between the instigational and the modeling functions of instructions. Instructions are most likely to produce correct performances when they both activate a person to respond and describe the requisite behaviors and the manner in which they must be executed. Little would be gained, for example, by simply ordering a person who has had no prior contact with cars to drive an automobile. In studies comparing the relative efficacy of instructions and verbal modeling (Masters & Branch, 1969), both types of influences produce their effects through verbal modeling and they differ only in the explicitness with which the necessary responses are defined. Greater performance gains are attained when desired behavior is clearly specified than when it must be inferred by observers from a few examples.

Explanations of modeling phenomena usually cease at the point where modeling stimuli are attributed informative functions. As shown earlier, the analysis must be extended beyond this level to explain how information conveyed by modeling stimuli is coded, the representational forms in which it is stored, and the process whereby representation guides action. Modeling stimuli, of course, do more than just convey information. They can also produce strong emotional and evaluative consequences that significantly affect both acquisition of new patterns of behavior and performance of existing ones (Bandura, 1971a).

Another issue requiring brief comment concerns the definition of response learning. Complex patterns of behavior are developed by organizing response elements that are present as products of maturation, or of prior observational learning and instrumental conditioning. Thus, for example, persons can produce a variety of elementary sounds as part of their natural endowment. By combining existing sounds one can create a novel and exceedingly complex verbal response such as *supercalifragilisticexpialidocious.*

Some writers (Aronfreed, 1969; Patterson, Littman, & Bricker, 1967) have questioned whether behavior formed through unique combinations of available elements represents response learning because the components already exist in subjects' repertoires. According to this line of reasoning, a pianist who has mastered a Beethoven piano concerto has learned nothing new because all the finger movements existed in his repertoire; and Beethoven cannot be credited with creating new symphonic music, he simply rearranged a few preexisting notes. Any behavior that has a very low or zero probability of occurrence under appropriate stimulus conditions qualifies as a novel response. Most new compound responses are composed of common behavioral elements.

Modeling influences can produce three differentiable types of effects in observers (Bandura & Walters, 1963). These include acquisition of new responses, weakening or strengthening of inhibitions over fully elaborated response patterns that already exist in observers' repertoires, and facilitation of performance of previously learned behaviors which are unencumbered by restraints and therefore the increased response is not attributable to disinhibitory processes. Controversies over observational learning often arise from failure to distinguish between modeling experiments primarily designed to produce learning effects from those intended to elucidate inhibitory or social facilitation effects. Observational response learning is most convincingly demonstrated in studies using specially constructed unique responses. It is extremely improbable, for example, that neologisms such as *lickitstickit* or *wetosmacko* (Bandura, Ross, & Ross, 1963) would ever emerge from subjects during an investigator's lifetime if these verbal responses were never modeled.

ALTERNATIVE EXPLANATIONS OF
NONREINFORCED MODELING

Among the various controversies over modeling theories that have arisen is the explanation of imitative behavior which is not explicitly reinforced. Baer and his associates (Baer, Peterson, & Sherman, 1967; Baer & Sherman, 1964) have interpreted the phenomenon, which they label "generalized imitation," in terms of conditioned reinforcement. This hypothesis assumes that positive reinforcement of matching responses endows similarity with rewarding properties that serve to maintain imitative responding.

In the experimental paradigm used to test this explanation of nonreinforced modeling, children are instructed by the model to imitate simple responses that he demonstrates sequentially, and each correct matching response is promptly reinforced. After a stable high rate of imitative behavior is established, a few similar responses that are never rewarded are randomly interspersed within a large changing set of reinforceable ones. Children generally imitate nonrewarded responses as long as accurate reproduction of other modeled behavior is positively reinforced.

Interpretation of nonreinforced modeling in terms of conditioned reinforcement is open to question on the basis of both conceptual and empirical considerations. First of all, the theory explains more than has ever been observed. If behavioral similarity is, in fact, inherently reinforcing, then people should display widespread modeling of all types of behavior exhibited by children, barbers, policemen, delinquents, professors, and others. In actuality, people tend to be highly selective in what they reproduce (Bandura, 1969b). A conditioned reinforcement interpretation would, therefore, have to include some contravening conditions to explain why people do not imitate indiscriminately everything that they may happen to observe.

As discussed more fully elsewhere (Bandura & Barab, 1971), the "generalized imitation" procedure includes a variety of extraneous rewards and coercive controls that result in multiple confounding of the effects of reinforcement variables on imitative response. Among the more forceful extraneous influences, the model commands the children to perform the demonstrated behavior and waits expectantly for aversively long intervals when they fail to respond imitatively. The strained silence can be terminated or attenuated only by their performing the requested matching responses. Escape from aversive conditions probably serves as a more powerful source of reinforcement maintaining imitative responding than the material rewards dispensed by the model.

Modeling often occurs in free-responding situations without explicit external reinforcement, and therefore the phenomenon requires explanation. According to the discrimination hypothesis, nonrewarded imitations persist in the absence of coercive control because individuals fail to discriminate differential reinforcement contingencies associated with diverse modeled behaviors. When a few nonrewarded modeled responses are randomly distributed in a large number that are consistently reinforced, the two sets of responses cannot easily be distinguished and are likely to be performed with similar frequency. If, on the other hand, the discriminative complexity of the modeling situation were reduced by having the model portray a series of reinforced responses, followed by the set of readily discriminable responses that are never rewarded, the observer would eventually recognize that the latter responses never produce positive outcomes and he would, in all likelihood, discontinue reproducing them. A discrimination hypothesis thus leads to a prediction which is opposite to that derived from the principle of secondary reinforcement. According to the acquired-reward interpretation, the longer that imitative responses are positively reinforced, the more strongly behavioral similarity is endowed with reinforcing properties and, consequently, the greater should be the resistance to extinction of nonrewarded matching responses. In contrast, a discrimination hypothesis would predict that the longer the differential reinforcement practices are continued, the more likely the observer is to distinguish between rewarded and nonrewarded imitative behaviors and to discontinue nonreinforced imitations.

To test this discrimination hypothesis, Bandura and Barab (1971) conducted an experiment that proceeded in the following manner: Young children participated in a modeling situation patterned after the generalized imitation paradigm except that coercive pressures for imitation were eliminated. During the initial procedure, the experimenter performed a series of motor responses and the children's matching performances were reinforced with food and approval until they displayed a high level of imitative responding. In the next phase, which measured generalization of imitation across models, the children were consistently reinforced for reproducing behavior of the first experimenter, but they were never rewarded for imitating a second experimenter who modeled a set of motor responses in the same sessions.

The third and final phase of the study was designed to test whether or not children would display discriminative imitation of the previously rewarding model, depending on the discriminability and functional value of his behavior. Accordingly, the first experimenter modeled the following three sets of responses:

1. Twenty of the original rewarded responses that continued to be reinforced;

2. Five nonrewarded responses having no conspicuous common attributes, randomly interspersed among the larger number of rewarded motor responses (It was hypothesized that the lack of distinguishing features and random presentation of these nonrewarded responses would, as in previous generalized imitation experiments, make it difficult for children to differentiate which responses were reinforced and which were not.); and

3. A second set of five nonrewarded responses consisting of vocalizations that would make them readily distinguishable. To increase their discriminability further, these responses were modeled one after the other in a block of trials rather than being randomly distributed throughout the rewarded items.

Figure 4 presents the mean imitative responses performed by children for different models and response classes on successive blocks of modeling trials. Inspection of the summary data shows that children readily discriminated between models in accordance with the prevailing reinforcement contingencies, and as sessions progressed, they rapidly decreased imitating the model who never reinforced matching behavior. Additional confirmation of the discrimination hypothesis is provided by data from the third phase, during which children continued to imitate both the rewarded matching responses and the set of indistinguishable nonreinforced responses at an equally high level, but they progressively reduced imitating the discriminable set of nonrewarded vocal responses (Figure 4). The evidence thus supports the view that, when extraneous social control is removed, persistence of nonreinforced matching behavior primarily reflects ambiguity about response consequences rather than acquired reward value of behavioral similarity.

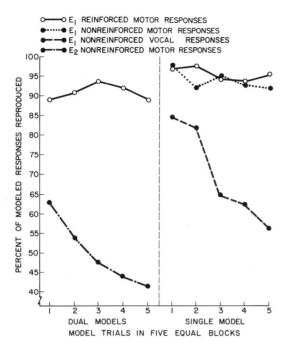

FIG. 4. Percent of modeled responses reproduced by children on successive blocks of modeling trials as a function of differential reinforcement for matching performances based on model characteristics and topography of the responses. E_1 refers to the model who rewarded imitations of twenty motor responses; E_2 refers to the model who never reinforced children for reproducing his behavior (Bandura & Barab, 1971).

Some of the children did not show differential imitation either across models or over classes of responses. A postexperimental inquiry revealed that these children generally recognized the differential reinforcement contingencies, but they did not act on their knowledge owing to erroneous expectations that nonimitation might be disapproved ("I am supposed to"), or that ignored imitations would eventually be rewarded ("I thought if I kept trying lots of times, he might get used to it and start up giving candy like the lady did"). Still others performed some nonrewarded behavior to confirm their hypotheses about the responses required to obtain reinforcement ("Sometimes I'd do it and sometimes not to see if I'd get any candy").

The implication of the overall findings is that if one wished to produce indiscriminate imitation, rather than depend on an inherent reinforcement mechanism to do the job, one would have to reinforce in a consistent manner imitation of different models performing diverse behaviors in varied settings. Such an outcome would not only be exceedingly difficult to achieve and even harder to maintain under the highly variable contingencies of everyday life, but since adaptive functioning requires discriminative responding, it would often create adverse consequences for undiscerning imitatees.

In several experiments reported by Steinman (1970a, 1970b), in which each modeled response was preceded by a command to the child to reproduce the demonstrated behavior, children imitated nonreinforced responses that they discriminated when no other alternatives were available. Discriminative responding is, of course, unlikely to emerge when subjects are commanded to respond alike to stimuli that are correlated with reinforcement and those that are not. When strong coercive control is superimposed on a differential reinforcement schedule, one would expect children to perform the demanded behavior regardless of whether or not it might later be rewarded. Steinman's research provides a convincing demonstration that instructional control can override the effects of differential reward for imitation in the paradigm widely used to study nonreinforced imitation. However, the findings have little bearing on the more important question of whether failure to discriminate differential consequences accounts for persistence of nonrewarded imitations under conditions in which modeled behavior is rarely, if ever, preceded by commands for immediate imitation.

When children were given choices between imitating reinforceable and nonreinforceable modeled responses (Steinman, 1970b), they initially exhibited a relatively high rate of nonrewarded imitations but gradually decreased such performances in succeeding modeling trials. Moreover, nonrewarded imitations were performed at a much higher level when they were topographically similar to the reinforced demonstrations than when they differed from them. This pattern of results, from the few cases studied, lends further support to the discrimination hypothesis.

The preceding comments are not meant to imply that all imitative behavior is exclusively under the joint control of discriminative stimuli and external reinforcement. Imitative behavior can be rendered partially independent of its external consequences. It is important to distinguish,

however, between response similarity as an automatic conditioned reinforcer and self-reinforcement of one's own performances. There is a
growing body of evidence (Bandura, 1971a, 1971c) that human behavior is
extensively under self-reinforcement control. In this type of self-regulatory
system, people set themselves certain performance standards and respond
to their own behavior in self-rewarding and self-punishing ways in accordance with their self-imposed demands. For this reason, response similarity is not invariably rewarding. People are inclined to respond self-
approvingly, and thereby reinforce their own efforts, whenever they
achieve close matches to meritorious performances. On the other hand,
equally close matches to devalued behaviors are likely to evoke self-punishing reactions and are therefore not repeated.

"Generalized imitation" might be more accurately designated as
generalization of imitative responses, which is largely regulated by discriminability of stimuli signifying probable consequences, by prior history of
selective reinforcement of imitative performances, and by subjective
reinforcement contingencies derived by individuals from other informative
cues. These influences control imitative behavior primarily through anticipated consequences of prospective actions that may or may not accurately
reflect objective conditions of reinforcement. As previously noted, in
everyday life some imitative behavior is undoubtedly self-maintained in
the absence of external reinforcement through self-rewarding reactions to
one's own skillful reproductions of personally valued activities.

In this brief presentation I have touched on some of the directions
in which modeling theory has developed since Richard Walters and I began
work in this area. It is evident from the innumerable citations in the
psychological literature to Richard's contributions and from the topics
discussed by the members of the present memorial symposium that his
influence lives on in the research activities of countless students and
colleagues.

REFERENCES

Aronfreed, J. The concept of internalization. In D. A. Goslin (Ed.), *Handbook of
    socialization theory and research.* Chicago: Rand McNally, 1969. Pp. 263-323.
Baer, D. M., Peterson, R. F., & Sherman, J. A. The development of imitation by
    reinforcing behavioral similarity to a model. *Journal of the Experimental
    Analysis of Behavior,* 1967, **10** , 405-416.

Baer, D. M., & Sherman, J. A. Reinforcement control of generalized imitation in young children. *Journal of Experimental Child Psychology,* 1964, **1,** 37-49.

Bandura, A. Influence of models' reinforcement contingencies on the acquisition of imitative responses. *Journal of Personality and Social Psychology,* 1965, **1,** 589-595.

Bandura, A. *Principles of behavior modification.* New York: Holt, 1969. (a)

Bandura, A. Social-learning theory of identificatory processes. In D. A. Goslin (Ed.), *Handbook of socialization theory and research.* Chicago: Rand McNally, 1969. Pp. 213-262. (b)

Bandura, A. Vicarious and self-reinforcement processes. In R. Glaser (Ed.), *The nature of reinforcement.* New York: Academic Press, 1971. Pp. 228-278. (a)

Bandura, A. Analysis of modeling processes. In A. Bandura (Ed.), *Psychological modeling.* Chicago: Aldine-Atherton, 1971. Pp. 1-67. (b)

Bandura, A. *Social learning theory.* New York: General Learning Press, 1971. (c)

Bandura, A., & Barab, P. G. Conditions governing nonreinforced imitation. *Developmental Psychology,* 1971, **5,** 244-255.

Bandura, A., Grusec, J. E., & Menlove, F. L. Observational learning as a function of symbolization and incentive set. *Child Development,* 1966, **37,** 499-506.

Bandura, A., & Harris, M. B. Modification of syntactic style. *Journal of Experimental Child Psychology,* 1966, **4,** 341-352.

Bandura, A., & Jeffery, R. The role of symbolic coding and rehearsal in observational learning. Unpublished manuscript, Stanford Univ., 1971.

Bandura, A., & McDonald, F. J. The influence of social reinforcement and the behavior of models in shaping children's moral judgements. *Journal of Abnormal and Social Psychology,* 1963, **67,** 274-281.

Bandura, A., & Mischel, W. Modification of self-imposed delay of reward through exposure to live and symbolic models. *Journal of Personality and Social Psychology,* 1965, **2,** 698-705.

Bandura, A., Ross, D., & Ross, S. A. A comparative test of the status envy, social power, and secondary reinforcement theories of identificatory learning. *Journal of Abnormal and Social Psychology,* 1963, **67,** 527-534.

Bandura, A., & Walters, R. H. *Social learning and personality development.* New York: Holt, 1963.

Dubanoski, R., & Parton, D. Imitation without a model. Paper presented at the Eastern Psychological Association meeting, Washington, 1968.

Foss, B. M. Mimicry in mynas (Gracula religiosa): A test of Mowrer's theory. *British Journal of Psychology,* 1964, **55,** 85-88.

Fouts, G. T., & Parton, D. A. Imitation: Effects of movement and static events. *Journal of Experimental Child Psychology,* 1969, **8,** 118-126.

Gerst, M. S. Symbolic coding processes in observational learning. *Journal of Personality and Social Psychology,* 1971, **19,** 7-17.

Gewirtz, J. L. Mechanisms of social learning: Some roles of stimulation and behavior in early human development. In D. A. Goslin (Ed.), *Handbook of socialization theory and research.* Chicago: Rand McNally, 1969.

Lovaas, O. I., Schreibman, L., Koegel, R., & Rehm, R. Selective responding by autistic children to multiple sensory input. *Journal of Abnormal Psychology,* 1972, in press.

Luchins, A. S., & Luchins, E. H. Learning a complex ritualized social role. *Psychological Record,* 1966, **16,** 177-187.

Masters, J. C., & Branch, M. N. Comparison of the relative effectiveness of instructions, modeling, and reinforcement procedures for inducing behavior change. *Journal of Experimental Psychology,* 1969, **80,** 364-368.

Michael, D. N., & Maccoby, N. Factors influencing the effects of student participation on verbal learning from films: Motivating versus practice effects, "feedback," and overt versus covert responding. In A. A. Lumsdaine (Ed.), *Student response in programmed instruction.* Washington, D. C.; National Academy of Sciences-National Research Council, 1961. Pp. 271-293.

Miller, N. E., & Dollard, J. *Social learning and imitation.* New Haven: Yale Univ. Press, 1941.

Patterson, G. R., Littman, R. A., & Bricker, W. Assertive behavior in children: A step toward a theory of aggression. *Monographs of the Society for Research in Child Development,* 1967, **32,** (5, Whole No. 113).

Steinman, W. M. Generalized imitation and the discrimination hypothesis. *Journal of Experimental Child Psychology,* 1970, **10,** 79-99. (a)

Steinman, W. M. The social control of generalized imitation. *Journal of Applied Behavior Analysis,* 1970, **3,** 159-167. (b)

Warden, C. J., Fjeld, H. A., & Koch, A. M. Imitative behavior in the Cebus and Rhesus monkeys. *Journal of Genetic Psychology,* 1940, **56,** 311-322.

Wasserman, L. Discrimination learning and development of learning sets in autistic children. Unpublished doctoral dissertation, Univ. of California, Los Angeles, 1968.

chapter 4

Imitation: Arguments for a Developmental Approach[1] | *Willard W. Hartup and Brian Coates*

This chapter is a rather odd tribute to Richard Walters. The oddity derives from our intention to raise some questions which are oblique, if not actually counter, to the main themes found in Walters' work on imitation.

In large measure, Walters was concerned with the problem of acquisition—that is, with behavioral acquisition deriving from observation of social models. Along with Professor Bandura, he argued cogently for a distinction between imitative acquisition and imitative performance. This distinction, however, continues to plague students of learning, and it has been no more adequately clarified with respect to observational learning than with respect to learning in general. Overall, however, Walters was

[1]A preliminary statement of the ideas contained in this paper was presented at the Miami University Symposium on Social Behavior, Oxford, Ohio, November 1, 1968. The proceedings of that symposium were published by Academic Press under the title *Early Experiences and the Processes of Socialization,* edited by R. Hoppe, G. A. Milton, and E. Simmel, 1970.

deeply concerned with the processes whereby the behavior of human beings changes as a function of observing the behavior of other persons. In one of his last papers, he summarized the theory which he (and Professor Bandura) felt most closely fits this type of behavioral acquisition:

> ... all observational learning may be encompassed within an analysis which requires only that stimuli be presented in conjunction and their association is, in some sense, "registered" within the memory "storage" of the organism. Presumably, neurophysiological and biochemical events are ultimately involved in the "registration" process, although too little is as yet known about these to aid much in the prediction of behavior. There is, however, sufficient evidence to support the view that, as a result of contiguous presentation, sensory experiences become "chained" in such a way that the re-presentation of a stimulus can elicit imaginal re-presentations of associated stimuli and that the perceptual-cognitive structures that are thus evoked may serve to guide behavior. In a sense, this theoretical position is not greatly different from that of the British empiricist philosophers ... except that we are now in a much better position, technically and methodologically, to investigate conditions under which "chaining" may occur [Walters, 1968, pp. 11-12].

Such a theory, although far from complete, has considerable viability with respect to the acquisition problem. Other theories may also be viable; our purpose is not to dissect them. Rather, our purpose here is to suggest that, in addition to acquisition, developmental psychologists should be equally concerned with the maintenance and transfer of imitation; further, that the analysis of these processes must include organismic changes in children of a variety of types. Consequently, there should be an increased concern with the imitative repertoire in children: (1) as this repertoire changes over time and (2) as this repertoire varies according to the situational context. There is no reason, either theoretical or methodological, for refraining longer from a full-scale attack on developmental problems in the study of imitation.

Interestingly, some of the earliest child work on imitation was ontogenetic in nature. This work showed clearly that early imitative behavior changes in concert with other changes taking place in the child. We recently discovered a monograph by Martha Guernsey, perhaps long familiar to some of you, which was published in 1928. Her results go to the heart of the matter. The study of 200 children between the ages of 2 and 21 months showed that actions "imitated" during this period are correlated with age, and that "first imitations" involve motoric and verbal responses appearing in the child's repertoire independent of imitation itself. That is, the infant appears to imitate "what he can do already." No child imitated before the age of 9.5 weeks; the earliest imitation involved mouth movements. Note here that Charlotte Bühler (1930) included imitative items in her infant scales at every level throughout the first two years. She included imitation of facial movements at month 3 (pursing the lips), imitation of forehead wrinkling at month 4, and sticking out the tongue at month 5. Imitation of limb movements and of sounds were inserted in these scales only at later points.

Next, note that Piaget (1951), in his discussions of imitation as the quintessence of accomodation, also described the first systematic imitations of the baby as involving behaviors already in the repertoire. Key later events, occurring in the second year, consist of spontaneously copying "new" behavior chains (it remains unclear what constitutes "new" behavior) and reproducing the model's actions when the model is no longer present. This latter event is sometimes called "delayed" or "deferred" imitation. Incidentally, Mary Shirley (1933) also mentioned the emergence of deferred imitation in her description of the second year of life.

These observations have been eclipsed by recent social learning analyses of imitation. Little attention has been paid to the developmental status of the subject (e.g., children's changing modes of responding to the environment) in recent analyses of the imitation problem. On the contrary, most contemporary research on children's imitation has been devoted to the study of variables that influence the functional relation between a given set of stimuli (including the behavior of a social model) and matching responses in children *at some one selected age level.* These studies assist greatly in the analysis of some developmental problems (e.g., socialization), but in themselves they do not resemble the developmental analyses of imitation to be found in either the work of Freud or the work of Piaget. Some investigators, including Robert Sears (e.g., Sears, 1957), have approached the problems of childhood imitation from a social learning view which is simultaneously a developmental view. But the bulk of research concerning children's imitation, from Miller and Dollard (1941) to Bandura and Walters (1963), has primarily been concerned with the "strengthening or weakening of stimulus-response functions." The yield from this effort consists of principles that undoubtedly have considerable trans-age applicability, but it is becoming increasingly apparent that qualifications must be placed on many of them.

Take, for example, Bandura's hypothesis (Bandura, Grusec, & Menlove, 1966) that appropriate mediational activity (i.e., correctly labeling the actions of a social model during observation of him) facilitates observational learning. A developmental question can be raised here. Does the relation between representational behavior and observational learning hold across all ages from infancy through adulthood? First, a minimum level of perceptual-representational capacity would seem necessary in order for imitation to occur, particularly if it is of the deferred or delayed type. But also, there appear to be developmental transpositions occurring in children between the preschool years (3 to 5) and the elementary school years (6 to 8) in the degree to which various types of mediators are spontaneously produced and effectively used (Flavell, Beach, & Chinsky, 1966). Thus, manipulations of mediational activity may differentially affect children's imitation at different age levels. This possibility has not been recognized in most recent research dealing with this problem.

A recent study by Coates and Hartup (1969) in an exception. We were interested in whether representational differences (i.e., verbalization) might account for age differences in observational learning between 4- and 7-year olds. In order to test this hypothesis, the children watched a movie, similar to one devised by Bandura, Grusec, and Menlove (1966), which showed a man performing a number of relatively novel behaviors such as building towers in unique ways, tossing a bean bag about, and so forth. The children watched the model under three conditions:

1. Induced verbalization: The subject was told how to describe the model's actions during exposure (i.e., he repeated the experimenter's verbalization about the model's behavior).

2. Free verbalization: The subject was asked to describe the model's actions in his own words during exposure.

3. Passive observation: No instructions related to verbalizing were given to the subject. All children were told that after the film they would be expected to show what the man in the movie had done.

Following some of Flavell's recent thinking (Flavell, Beach, & Chinsky, 1966), we believed that the younger children would not spontaneously produce relevant verbalizations in the no instruction condition but that the older children would. We believed, though, that if the younger subjects were *helped* to produce relevant verbalizations, that their task performance would be enhanced. Thus, we predicted the following:

1. The 4-year olds would show greater observational learning when verbalizations were induced than when the child passively observed the model;

2. The 4-year olds in the free verbalization condition (who would presumably make fewer relevant verbalizations than the induced subjects) would perform at an intermediate level; and

3. There would be no differences in observational learning among 7-year olds in the three experimental conditions—they would presumably produce relevant verbalizations spontaneously.

The results confirmed all of the predictions except that, among the older subjects, free verbalization produced *less* observational learning than either the induction procedure of passive observation. Although free verbalization in this study *reduced* observational learning among the older children, Bandura and his colleagues had earlier found that such verbalization *facilitated* observational learning among subjects who were similar in age to this portion of our sample. The discrepancy in the two sets of results for 7-year olds is still unclear. The Coates and Hartup study, however, strongly suggests that developmental differences in the production of relevant verbalizations is one factor accounting for differences in observational learning between 7-year olds and 4-year olds. After all, the induction of accurate verbalizations did not facilitate observational learning among the older children, but it clearly did among the 4-year olds.

There are very few studies, such as this one, which have explored the interaction among stimulus inputs, developmental status, and observational learning. The reasons for this paucity of developmental research are numerous. For one thing, we have needed large amounts of nondevelopmental, variable-oriented research as a prerequisite for research on the complicated developmental problems in this area. Social learning theory, which has guided most of the recent imitation research, has had an inherent elegance for dealing with acquisition problems, a traditional emphasis upon experimental methodologies, and a cathexis for parametric study of the variables relating to behavior change. These qualities have had something to do with the ascendance of social learning theory in research on children's imitation. Overall, we believe that this tradition in imitation research has been sanguine: Perhaps no other theory could have pushed the study of children's observational learning and imitation so far, so fast.

We think, however, that we are sufficiently sophisticated in our functional analyses of imitation to begin in earnest the study of imitative development in children. The problem of "first imitations," the production of "generalized" imitation, and the role of imitation in the socialization of the child cannot fully be understood until we do. For this purpose, we need sophisticated analyses of the modeling problem focusing on a wide variety of temperamental and cognitive vicissitudes, as these interact with contingencies of exposure to models in determining children's tendencies to imitate. Such research will facilitate our accounting for some of the problems we have listed (e.g., the emergence of "first imitations"), but it should also increase the practical usefulness of our knowledge concerning imitation with respect to child rearing, childhood education, and psychotherapy with children. The case to be made for developmental research on imitation is, for us, not a theoretical issue but a question of values.

FIRST IMITATIONS

With these remarks as background, let us consider briefly the status of research on "first imitations." Within the past several years, reinforcement psychologists have devoted increasing attention to this problem. One of the best accounts from this viewpoint, of the acquisition and maintenance of first imitations is provided by J. L. Gewirtz:

> The first imitative responses must occur by chance, through direct physical assistance, or through direct training (with shaping or fading procedures applied by a reinforcing agent to occurring responses). When such responses occur, they are strengthened and maintained by direct extrinsic reinforcement from environmental agents. After several imitative responses become established in this manner, a class of diverse but *functionally equivalent* behaviors is acquired and maintained by extrinsic reinforcement on an intermittent schedule. Differences in response content of the imitative behaviors are thought to play a minimal role as long as the responses are members of the imitative response class as defined functionally by *reinforcing agents* [Gewirtz & Stingle, 1968, p. 379].

Thus, Gewirtz and Stingle hypothesized that matching responses first occur by chance, response strength (rate of occurrence) of matching responses increases as a function of intermittent reinforcement, and even-

tually a sufficient number of reinforced responses occurs so that a generalized imitative repertoire (relatively free of reinforcement) is built up.

The experiments supporting these hypotheses (e.g., Baer & Sherman,
1965) have not involved the direct study of babies. The relevant experiments have been carried out with children who show evidence of little or
no imitative behavior, but the subjects have been feeble-minded or schizophrenic children. These experiments have consistently shown that children
having little or no imitative behavior in their initial repertoires eventually
emit frequent imitations if reinforcement occurs contingently with respect
to responses that have been rigged to match those of a social model. The
rigging of a match in these studies has usually involved "prompting." That
is, the experimenter guides the subject through the motoric aspects of the
desired behavior during the beginning of the experimental phase of the
study.

A number of questions may be raised concerning the relation of
this literature to the problem of imitative origins. First, there are obvious
differences between infancy, the period in which matching behavior is first
manifested in normal children, and the psychological status of the older
retarded or psychotic child. Contingencies of reinforcement may well be
related to the increase in social imitation found in normal infancy. It may
also be necessary, however, to bring other variables and other hypotheses
into our analysis in order to account for the emergence of the *particular*
matches that occur during babyhood. Attentional processes, conceptual
abilities, and motivational factors may be involved, in important ways, in
the infant's first imitations that differ from the ways in which these
processes impinge on first imitations in the retarded or schizophrenic
child.

With respect to attention, for example, Valentine (1930-31) described
involuntary imitation as "the monopolization of attention by some fascinating impression." Crawford and Spence (1939) also argued that the
impact of the social chimpanzee model is largely in attention-setting.
Considering other knowledge concerning attentional processes in infancy,
we cannot believe that *all* that is involved in producing first imitations is
contingent reinforcement or contiguous stimulation involving the behavior
of social models.

Second, there is need of an assessment of the role of prompts in first
imitations. Prompts of the kind used in present experimental work may be
relatively unimportant in the infant's first imitations. Accident may be

involved in eliciting early matches, although we are inclined to believe that most first matches are semiaccidents, at best. In fact, the first instances of matched behavior in infancy are most likely to be outcomes of the deliberate matching of the child *by the parent*. Parents may occasionally manipulate the child's motor responses so as to produce a match, but we doubt that this is practiced extensively. For this reason parental matching should be studied as a determinant of first imitations in the child. Innate preprogramming of some aspects of parental behavior may underly the provision of some of those stimuli (such as mouth movements and facial expressions) that produce early matches by the baby. This hypothesis cannot be ruled out if one is interested in the overall question of imitative origins. Parental learning histories, of course, may also be relevant antecedents of the child's first imitations.

At any rate, one sees immediately why the problem of first imitations is so complex. To us, the antecedents and mechanisms producing these first matches are key problems for developmental psychologists although such problems may be of limited interest to those who are mainly concerned with understanding the processes of social *learning*. We do not believe, however, that the natural history of imitative behavior is entirely a reflection of the early reinforcement history nor that first imitations come about solely by chance or accident.

Reinforcement or contiguity theory may effectively account for the strengthening of imitative stimulus-response functions once matching begins to occur, but studies involving parent-infant interaction are needed to test this assertion. Research dealing with the first imitations of disturbed, non-imitating older children constitutes a promising empirical base from which to pursue the origins of imitation in infant development, but we must also study the infant himself. Those imitations that can be produced in retarded and schizophrenic children may not, even with extensive training, be similar to the imitations which one observes in normal 1- or 2-year-olds. Lovaas has clearly indicated his awareness of this problem in several publications (e.g., Lovaas, 1967). Thus, we come back to the possibility that spontaneous imitation in children depends not only on contingencies but also involves an interplay among conceptual-perceptual capacities and social inputs. We doubt that "generalized imitation" (a kind of semienduring trait in the child) is a construct that will lead us very far in accounting for the complex variation across situations, models, and behaviors that is characteristic of imitative behavior in normal children.

GENERALIZED IMITATION

Let us briefly look at the question of generalized imitation. Naturalistic observation reveals that children readily imitate new models (e.g., models that are not involved in the precipitation of first imitations) and also, that they imitate old models in new situations. These phenomena bring to mind the concepts of stimulus and response generalization. Both concepts have been used in theorizing about imitation, but there have been very few studies of "generalized modeling." Actually, it is difficult to apply traditional generalization paradigms to the existing data. Specifically, what is generalized? In imitation, is the relevant dimension a stimulus one or a response one? In one of the Lovaas studies of schizophrenic children (Lovaas, Berberich, Perloff, & Scheaffer, 1966), the subjects were tested for "response" generalization by presenting them with Norwegian words. Each word was presented many times, but no reinforcement was given for imitation. However, other imitative behaviors were reinforced, including imitation of interpolated English words. There was an increase over trials in the number of imitations of the Norwegian words. Note here that the modeling stimulus (which includes not only the person of the model but also his behavior) varies from training to test trials; that is, he displayed different characteristics: English speech in the training trials, Norwegian speech in the test trials. Is the transfer, then, stimulus or response generalization? This problem is pervasive in the small literature dealing with generalization of imitation, and makes it difficult to conceptualize the issues when we consider generalization across situations, across models, and across time in natural socialization settings.

Perhaps more important than this conceptual difficulty, however, is that little is known except that generalized modeling is demonstrable. The research, including the early work by Miller and Dollard, as well as the more recent work of Bandura and Lovaas, extends across a very narrow range of stimulus and response parameters. There are a number of questions that need to be answered at this time. What conditions affect the extent to which imitation generalizes? Would training of imitation on partial reinforcement schedules result in different generalization gradients from training with continuous reinforcement? What are the stimulus dimensions which govern generalized imitation in natural settings? Is generalization similar at different age levels? Generalization to model-absent settings, for example, may not occur before the second year, but may occur readily thereafter. Also, studies of generalization in older children suggest that generalization functions may vary according to the developmental status of the child.

One widespread assumption in naturalistic studies of identification is that propensities to imitate, first established vis á vis parent models, generalize to teachers and peers. We have no data concerning this hypothesis. As we have said, the range of stimuli used in experiments on the generalization of children's imitation has been extremely narrow. Obviously, much research is needed, both experimental and naturalistic, concerning the generalization of imitation. In particular, we know little concerning the acquisition of discriminations that result in the imitation of some models and some behaviors but not others.

DEVELOPMENT DURING CHILDHOOD

Age differences in children's imitation have been analyzed in only about ten experimental studies.[2] The youngest children involved in these studies were 3-year olds, and the oldest were 18 years of age. One can ask several questions of this literature, sparse as it is. First, do the results show a strengthening of generalized imitation during childhood? The answer is: "We cannot tell." The studies indicate that the occurrence of significant age differences in children's imitation depends on the task involved. There seem to be increases in imitation with age on complex tasks which have involved explicit instructions to imitate. On the other hand, few age differences of any kind occur on relatively simple tasks when no instructions to imitate are given. (So-called conformity behavior is a clear exception to this latter statement.) This state of affairs suggests some of the limitations inherent in the concept of generalized imitation or, at the very least, that we face serious methodological hurdles in studying the transfer and maintenance problem developmentally.

We can, however, ask whether age differences in children's imitations reveal changes in developmental status. Assume, for the moment, that generalized imitation quickly asymptotes in early childhood and, from then on, that task differences in imitation reflect the outcomes of discrimination training or other developmental changes. The ten existing studies

[2] For a review of these studies see Hartup and Coates (1970).

do not cover much behavioral territory, but the patterning of age differences seems, indeed, to reflect changes in developmental status. One of the more interesting studies in this area is by Wapner and Cirillo (1967). They found an increase from age 8 to age 18 in the frequency with which children copied exactly the model's display of left-right relations. At the same time, the frequency of inexact or "wrong" imitations declined. Such data suggest that cognitive skills place a variety of constraints upon imitative behavior. Put another way, the disorderly age changes in imitation revealed by present research may have considerable significance as reflections of basic changes in the manner in which the child conceptualizes and views the world. And, incidentally, such findings may have relatively little to do with the strengthening or weakening of generalized imitation as such.

We think, however, that age differences of the type mentioned here are of considerable interest to those who are primarily interested in imitation as a *process*. It appears to us that imitation is intertwined with a variety of cognitive and motivational changes taking place during childhood. It may serve no useful purpose to try to tear apart the concept of imitation from other aspects of the child's cognitive and social functioning. Such tearing apart may actually obscure the developmental properties of the phenomenon in which we are interested.

In sum, we have very poor understanding of the interactions among stimulus inputs, developmental factors, and observation of models in modifying the behavior of children. We have not, in most experiments in this field, touched the *developmental* aspects of such protean theories as those presented by Freud and Piaget. Bits of those theories have provided the base for productive work concerning the factors that influence children's imitation, but the epigenetic character of children's imitations (conceived in both of these theories) has been left virtually untouched by research workers. The few extant *developmental* studies provide a beginning for research of this sort, but the interplay between changes in attentional, motivational, and cognitive functioning and imitation in childhood is presently one large unmapped area. Also, fascinating prospects lie ahead in developmental research that deals with the interrelations among attachment and dependency, role taking, and imitative performance — again if we approach these problems from a developmental standpoint.

The contributions of Richard Walters have brought us to the point from which such studies can begin. His work will remain as a superb example of the process-oriented research needed to give us some idea of where to look in our efforts to understand the role played by imitation in childhood socialization. Some of our effort must be redirected at this point, however, if we are to give an adequate accounting of either the ontogenesis of imitative behavior or the manner in which such behavior is embedded in the child's general socialization. And this redirection must involve reference to a variety of age-related changes in children as these furnish a context for exposure to social models.

REFERENCES

Baer, D. M., & Sherman, J. A. Reinforcement control of generalized imitation in young children. *Journal of Experimental Child Psychology.* 1965, **1**, 37-49.
Bandura, A., Grusec, J., & Menlove, F. Observational learning as a function of symbolization and incentive set. *Child Development,* 1966, **37**, 499-507.
Bandura, A., & Walters, R. H. *Social learning and personality development.* New York: Holt, 1963.
Bühler, C. *The first year of life.* New York: John Day, 1930.
Coates, B., & Hartup, W. W. Age and verbalization in observational learning. *Developmental Psychology,* 1969, **1**, 556-562.
Crawford, M. P., & Spence, K. W. Observational learning of discrimination problems by chimpanzees. *Journal of Comparative and Physiological Psychology,* 1939, **27**, 133-147.
Flavell, J. H., Beach, D. R., & Chinsky, J. M. Spontaneous verbal rehearsal in a memory task as a function of age. *Child Development,* 1966, **37**, 283-299.
Gewirtz, J. L., & Stingle, K. G. Learning of generalized imitation as the basis for identification. *Psychological Review,* 1968, **75**, 374-397.
Guernsey, M. Eine genetische studie uber nachahnung. *Zeitschrift fur Psychologie,* 1928, **107**, 105-178.
Hartup, W. W., & Coates, B. The role of imitation in childhood socialization. In R. A. Hoppe, G. A. Milton, & E. C. Simmel. *Early experiences and the processes of socialization.* New York: Academic Press, 1970. Pp. 109-142.
Lovaas, O. I. A behavior therapy approach to the treatment of childhood schizophrenia. In J. P. Hill (Ed.), *Minnesota symposia on child psychology.* Vol. I. Minneapolis: Univ. of Minnesota Press, 1967. Pp. 108-159.
Lovaas, O. I., Berberich, J. P., Perloff, B. F., & Schaeffer, B. Acquisition of imitative speech in schizophrenic children. *Science,* 1966, **151**, 705-707.
Miller, N. E., & Dollard, J. *Social learning and imitation.* New Haven, Conn.: Yale Univ. Press, 1941.
Piaget, J. *Play, dreams, and imitation in childhood.* New York: Norton, 1951.

Sears, R. R. Identification as a form of behavior development. In D. B. Harris (Ed.). *The concept of development.* Minneapolis: Univ. of Minnesota Press, 1957. Pp. 149-161.

Shirley, M. *The first two years.* Vol. II. Minneapolis: Univ. of Minnesota Press, 1933.

Valentine, C. W. The psychology of imitation with special reference to early childhood. *British Journal of Psychology,* 1930-31, **21,** 105-132.

Walters, R. H. Some conditions facilitating the occurrence of imitative behavior. In E. C. Simmel, R. Hoppe, & G. A. Milton (Eds.), *Imitation and social facilitation.* Boston: Allyn Bacon, 1968. Pp. 7-30.

Wapner, S., and Cirillo, L. Imitation of a model's hand movements: Age changes in transposition of left-right relations. *Child Development,* 1968, **39,** 887-894.

chapter 5

Punishment and "Reasoning" in the Development of Self-Control | *J. Allan Cheyne*[1]

Dick Walters' philosophy was that research could be conducted most fruitfully when guided by theory. This, however, did not detract from the realization that one was trying to understand a phenomenon as well as demonstrating the appropriateness of a particular theoretical orientation. Dr. Walters had become particularly pleased with the paradigm with which he had been dealing in the punishment studies but not because it had supported his initial theorizing. Quite the contrary, what pleased him so much was that the experimental setting allowed the child a great deal of freedom to expose the weakness of the original theoretical considerations thus providing clues for a better conceptualization from which to view behavior.

[1] This chapter was prepared while the author was an Ontario Mental Health Foundation Research Fellow at the University of Waterloo.

SOCIALIZATION AND SELF-CONTROL

To a considerable extent the concept of socialization may be considered as the development of increasing correspondence of the attitudes, values, and actions of individuals with socially defined norms or standards. Socialized self-control may be thought of as action (or refraining from action) that conforms to social norms in the absence of surveillance by social agents and, moreover, does so in the absence of concurrent reinforcements that might be presumed to maintain the behavior in question.

Much of the research that has been concerned with socialization has involved what might be termed "positive self-control" that is, performing actions specified by a norm. The subject of this paper is rather the dark side of the problem of socialization, that is, negative self-control: the inhibition of action proscribed by social rules. We will refer to this negative self-control as "resistance-to-deviation."

In considering the learning of such response inhibition, one immediately thinks of the disciplinary technique referred to as "punishment." Punishment has, in the child-rearing literature, received considerable attention and has been the subject of some study. Early discussions of punishment, however, seldom got beyond disputing or affirming the effectiveness of punishment for producing response inhibition. Until recently, there had been little work that expanded our knowledge of the effects on children's social behavior of variations in the most basic parameters of punishment, such as timing, intensity, and consistency. For example, any suggestions as to the effect of delayed punishment found their only empirical validation in studies involving animals or human subjects in extremely simple situations.

It is perhaps commonplace to suggest that the effects of variations in the parameters of punishment and rewards may change as our investigations move from the study of simple organisms in simple situations to more complex organisms in more complex situations as, for example, when a child is punished in the context of verbal instructions that may clarify or even change the meaning of punishment. It is obviously an important task of the developmentalist to determine with some precision the nature and extent of such changes.

In the socialization literature the verbal context in which punishment occurs in the parent-child interaction is usually referred to as "reasoning." Reasoning probably contains several kinds of significant information, such as: preferred alternate behaviors and salient features of the prohibited behavior, as well as providing cognitive structure in the sense that behavior is categorized and labeled for the child.

The research that will be reported here has attempted to do a number of things, three of which are as follows:

1. To determine whether variations in the parameters of punishment produce effects in children similar to those that have been found in lower animals when punishment is without accompanying instructions;

2. To determine what happens to these effects when certain kinds of verbalizations are brought into the situation;

3. To understand how such changes, if they are found, have been produced.

TIMING AND INTENSITY OF PUNISHMENT

Research with animals has suggested that, other things being held constant, the effectiveness of punishment for producing response inhibition is a simple function of the intensity of punishment and of the temporal interval between the initiation of the response and the administration of punishment (e.g., Church, Raymond, & Beauchamp, 1967). Research with children has suggested that, under certain conditions, similar effects may be obtained. An illustrative experiment using a resistance-to-deviation paradigm is discussed here.

The basic procedure used in the studies presented throughout this paper can be described briefly at this point. The experiments were all conducted at the school in a mobile laboratory. Children, selected from kindergarten through grade 3 (no one study reported here combined data from more than two adjacent grade levels), were brought individually to the trailer by the experimenter. Each child was seated at a table on which toys were presented in pairs, and the child was required to make a selection from each pair (in various experiments the specific number of pairs varied although in any given experiment the number of pairs was constant across conditions). For certain selections the child received punishment in the form of a loud buzzer which was designed to be aversive but not upsetting or frightening. Subsequently, the circumstances were so contrived that the child was left alone with the punished toy(s) for a 15-minute period, and observers in an adjoining room recorded the child's interaction with the toy, a deviation being any physical contact with the punished object. From the observers' records it was possible to determine the *latency* of the first deviation and the *duration* (in seconds) of deviation during the test period.[2]

Intensity of punishment was manipulated simply by varying the intensity level of the buzzer, a high-intensity punishment involving approximately a 100 dB buzzer, and a low-intensity buzzer, approximately a 65-80 dB buzzer.

In manipulating the timing of punishment, early-punishment was delivered as the child's hand approached the selected toy and late-punishment was administered approximately 3 seconds after the child lifted the toy from the table.

Studies that have manipulated both variables in a factorial design have found that, *in the absence of instructions,* high-intensity punishment produces greater resistance-to-deviation than low-intensity punishment and early-punishment is similarly more effective than late-punishment (Cheyne, 1969; 1971; Cheyne & Walters, 1969; Parke, 1969). The relevant group means from one study are presented in Table 1.

Such findings as those in Table 1 have typically been explained in these studies by reference to two-factor learning theory (e.g., Mowrer, 1960a,b). According to this theory each component of a response sequence provides sensory feedback consisting of kinesthetic and proprioceptive cues. Punishment may, of course, be administered at any point in the response sequence and cause the association of resultant fear-motivated avoidance responses with cues from any component of the instrumental response. Presumably the greater the physical intensity of the punisher, the greater the magnitude of the associated negative affective ("fear") response. Moreover, punishment delivered at the initiation of a response will associate the fear responses with cues produced by acts initiating the response sequences relatively more closely than late punishment. Hence, subsequent initiation of the response sequence will generate associated incompatible avoidance responses more quickly in early punishment than in late punishment. If the avoidance responses are sufficient to

---

[2] A third measure (number of deviations) has been used in the past but will be ignored here because the measure has seldom provided information beyond that provided by latency and duration.

TABLE 1

MEANS OF LATENCY AND DURATION OF DEVIATION
FOR FOUR PUNISHMENT CONDITIONS[a]

Intensity of punishment		Timing of punishment	
		Early	Late
Latency			
	High	316.5	117.9
	Low	181.7	42.6
Duration			
	High	18.6	22.5
	Low	20.1	96.5

[a]From Cheyne, 1971.

terminate the instrumental response, the former responses will be rein-forced through fear reduction.

It is clear from observing the overt behavior of subjects in the experiment described that high-intensity punishment has a greater affec-tive impact than low-intensity punishment (Cheyne & Walters, 1969; Cheyne, Goyeche, & Walters, 1969; Leff, 1969). It is also clear from observing the overt behavior of subjects that early punishment has a greater affective impact than late punishment (Cheyne & Walters, 1969, 1970; Parke & Walters, 1967; Walters & Parke, 1968). In a study described earlier, the data for which is presented in Table 1, heart rate was moni-tored during and immediately following punishment and a beat-by-beat calculation of means for each condition is presented in Figure 1. To the extent that cardiac acceleration may be interpreted to reflect an affective response, the inferences to be drawn from the heart-rate data are com-pletely supportive of those drawn from the overt reactions of subjects. Specifically, it may be suggested that the *magnitude* of the affective reaction to punishment depends on both the physical intensity of the punisher and the temporal relation between the response and the punish-ment. That is, even a punishment of low-intensity may induce affectivity if it occurs during the initiation of a response, possibly because of interrup-tion effects (Cheyne, 1971; Mandler, 1964; Mandler & Watson, 1966). Thus, it seems reasonable at this point to conclude that, in the absence of reasoning, the strength of resistance-to-deviation is a fairly simple function of the level of negative affect associated with that behavior.

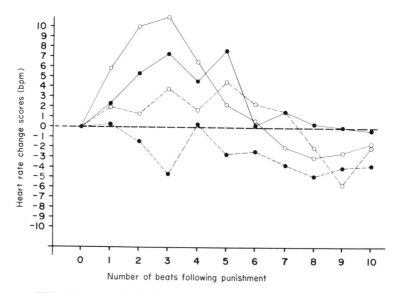

FIG. 1. Mean heart-rate change scores for each physical punishment condition for each of 10 beats following onset of buzzer. (Open circles represent high intensity; filled circles, low intensity; unbroken line, early punishment; broken line, late punishment.) From Cheyne (1971).

However, it is dubious that response inhibition thus mediated would be conducive to effective social behavior with all its subtleties. Indeed, field studies that have investigated the role of physical punishment in socialization have yielded weak and inconsistent findings. There seems little evidence that high-parental punitiveness leads to greater resistance-to-deviation than low-parental punitiveness, and in fact, the evidence often may be taken to suggest that the reverse is true. Sears and his associates (Sears, Maccoby, & Levin, 1957) for example, have not found punishment to be strongly related to resistance-to-deviation.[3] However, it is interesting to note that these investigators did find that frequent punishment accompanied by reasoning was reported as being more effective than frequent punishment without reasoning, or infrequent punishment with or

[3] We should note here that the concept of parental punitiveness tends to confound a number of dimensions, the effects of interactions among which are unknown. The problems involved in the interpretation of such data have been discussed by a number of writers (e.g., Walters & Parke, 1968).

without reasoning. Unfortunately, it is impossible, from data gathered in such survey studies, to determine which specific aspects of information conveyed by reasoning are instrumental in promoting subsequent resistance-to-deviation.

REASONING

In the laboratory one can investigate the modification of the effects of punishment by introducing or withholding instructions containing rather specific kinds of information. Perhaps the most fundamental and most essential information is that which specifies the forbidden response. It is an *explicit* statement of a rule of behavior. Instructions may also provide information that is more abstract and generalized and which may be of fundamental importance in advanced forms of self-control such as is contained in general statements of ethical or moral precepts. Thus, this latter kind of statement may be viewed as a superordinate proposition that, in some sense, "justifies" or "explains" the imposition of the behavior rule. Such verbalizations may be particularly important in generalizing behavior across situations that are superficially very different (Burton, 1963). Of course, we should note here that punishment itself contains some information. This point refers to what have been called the "cue properties" of punishment (e.g., Walters & Parke, 1968).

Thus, we may view the punishment situation as becoming more elaborated in terms of the amount of information available in the situation. Some examples of these forms of elaboration are illustrated in Table 2.

Although a number of studies have been performed using the resistance-to-deviation paradigm investigating the effects of such instructions, only one study has systematically investigated the relative effects of different levels of information as illustrated in Table 2 and using the examples given in Table 2. In this study children were required to choose one of a pair of toys and, having selected one, were presented with the first statement, the first two statements, or all three statements. The main results of this study are given in Figure 2. The first two graphs[4] represent the first-level elaboration, the next two the second-level, and the last one the third-

[4] Conditions P-C_1 and P-C_2 constituted control conditions containing nonrule verbalizations to assure that it was the specific content of the verbalizations that produced resistance-to-deviation.

TABLE 2

INCREASING ELABORATION OF THE PUNISHMENT SITUATION

	Punishment	Behavior rule	Norm statement
Affective reaction	Fear induction alerting		
Type of information available	Something wrong has been done	X is forbidden	X is a member of a class of forbidden behaviors
Examples	(That is bad)	Do not touch or play with that object	That belongs to someone else

level. In agreement with the findings of the Sears, Maccoby, & Levin (1957) study, punishment appears to become more effective with the addition of reasoning. Moreover, we can see that each kind of information is added to the total resistance-to-deviation.

As the child develops, his language skills and cognitive capacities increase, and hence one must conclude that reasoning techniques may therefore take on increasing importance in punishment episodes. Initially, for the preverbal child, reasoning, or instructions, should be quite ineffective for modifying the effects of punishment. However, later the child should be able to use the information contained in verbal statements accompanying punishment. At first, concrete information may be utilized, such as the specification of the punished response (behavior rule). Still later the child may utilize the more abstract kinds of information relating to social properties of the act (e.g., a property norm) that may raise the behavior rule to the level of a moral rule.[5]

[5] Strictly speaking the statement in Figure 2 illustrating the moral precept is not *itself* a statement of a moral rule. Rather, it is because of the nature of the information that the first-level, or behavior, rule becomes a second-level or moral rule. An explicit statement of the moral rule itself would be something to the effect that: "One does not play with toys that belong to someone else." The assumption is, of course, that the abstract moral rule is more relevant for older children in terms of controling their behavior. That this inference may indeed be correct is suggested by the decreased deviation of older (but not of younger) children under the most elaborated reasoning conditions.

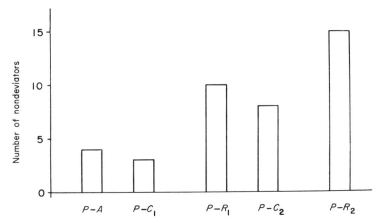

FIG. 2. Number of nondeviating subjects under each of three levels of structure ($P\text{-}A$, $P\text{-}R_1$, $P\text{-}R_2$) or control conditions ($P\text{-}C_1$, $P\text{-}C_2$).

In the study just discussed both kindergarten and grade 3 children were studied. There is reason to believe that kindergarten children are operating at a more concrete level both in terms of verbal control of motor responding (Luria, 1961) and in Piaget's terms of intellectual operations (Flavell, 1963) and, of particular interest here, also in terms of moral judgments (Kohlberg, 1963, 1964; Piaget, 1932). As we can see in Figure 3, the kindergarten children benefited from the first kind of verbal information but apparently not from the second, whereas the older children seemed to respond differentially to each level of elaboration. Hence, we may conclude that, although reasoning may modify the effects of punishment, the degree to which it does and the aspects of reasoning that are operative depend on the developmental level of the child.

INTERACTIONS

The introduction of cognitive factors into the punishment situation necessitates some modification of the basic theoretical framework suggested earlier that seemed to account for the data gathered in the more cognitively "barren" settings. Aronfreed (1965, 1968) has modified that framework by suggesting that anxiety may become associated with cognitive

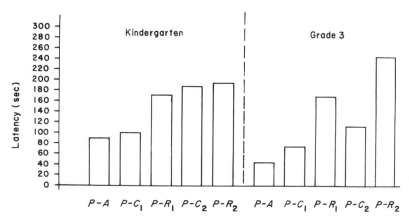

FIG. 3. Average latency of deviation for each of five conditions for kindergarten and for grade 3 children.

representations of verbalizations accompanying punishment. Such a framework implies that the effectiveness of punishment training for producing
resistance–to-deviation depends on a close temporal association between the
verbal mediator and affective reactions to punishment. Here conditioned
affective reactions are retained as the basic mediators of resistance-to-
deviation, but their potential as mediators of self-control in social situations is greatly expanded.

It is clear that, under certain conditions, instructions, or reasoning,
may enhance the effectiveness of punishment. It is a question of some
interest as to the conditions which optimize this enhancement. Related to
this question is the second main issue raised at the beginning of this paper:
How do instructions modify the effects of variations of the parameters of
punishment? A number of studies suggest that, although relatively short
delays of punishment may reduce its effectiveness for producing resistance-to-deviation, the addition of instructions may attenuate or eliminate
the effect (Aronfreed, 1965, 1966). One may ask what the limits of this
effect may be. How great a temporal gap may the instructions bridge? In
many real-life situations the delay between the commission of a deviant act
and punishment may be considerably greater than a few seconds, that is,
several hours in duration. One's immediate reaction to the effectiveness of
such punishment may be summed up in J. B. Watson's statement that

"The idea that a child's future bad behavior will be prevented by giving him a licking in the evening for something he did in the morning is ridiculous." A dissertation study done under Dr. Walters by Andres (1967) suggests, however, that instructions accompanying punishment (loud noise) may increase the effectiveness of punishment that has been delayed several hours. In this study children were allowed to play, in the experimenter's absence, with a toy that was designed to break when handled. The child broke the toy, of course, and was subsequently taken from the trailer by a confederate of the experimenter. Four hours later the experimenter returned the subject to the trailer and administered punishment. Under one condition the child was merely seated at the same table and punished. In other conditions children were required to reperform the deviant act, or view a video-recording of their earlier deviation, or to listen to the experimenter verbally describe their deviation. This last condition was especially effective for producing resistance-to-deviation. The actual group means are presented in Table 3. Thus, even relatively long delays between the deviant response and punishment may be spanned by procedures that restructure the situation for the child. Particularly, the results of this study suggest, in contrast to Aronfreed's suggestions, that a close relation between the intero- and exteroceptive stimuli accompanying deviation and punishment may be of less importance than the clear knowledge of what is and what is not prohibited behavior.

In addition to finding that the presence of instructions may modify the effects of punishment, we have also found that certain parameters of punishment may increase or decrease the salience of verbalizations accompanying punishment. In certain experiments we have found that delayed punishment followed by instructions was more effective than immediate

TABLE 3

MEANS OF LATENCY AND DURATION OF DEVIATIONS
FOR FOUR PUNISHMENT CONDITIONS

Condition	Latency	Duration
Minimal	200.47	142.40
Reperform	278.47	69.40
Film	489.53	23.67
Verbal	568.27	19.33

punishment followed by instructions. That is, rather than merely eliminating the timing effect, we have reversed it. Such an effect we feel to be of some importance in view of the fact that great emphasis has frequently been placed on the potential effects on social behavior of variations in the timing of punishment (e.g., Solomon, Turner, & Lessac, 1967).

The finding that the timing effect could, in fact, be reversed was really a serendipidous discovery. In an early study that attempted to manipulate timing and intensity of punishment independently, Parke & Walters (1967, experiment 3) found that although early punishment was more effective than late punishment under high-intensity punishment conditions, the reverse was true for low-intensity punishment conditions. Specifically, subjects under the low-intensity-late-punishment exhibited an unexpectedly high degree of resistance-to-deviation. In that study punishment was, under all conditions, followed by the statement by the experimenter, "that belongs to another boy". Follow-up studies have strengthened the conclusion that the presence or absence of instructions immediately following punishment is crucial in determining the direction of effects of timing and intensity (Cheyne & Walters, 1969; Parke, 1969). On the basis of studies reported earlier in this paper (although actually performed subsequently), such a verbalization could be expected to produce a marked increment in response suppression.

The question arises, however, as to why this was not so under the other three conditions. The answer to this question may be provided in Figure 1. Under either high-intensity or early-punishment conditions, subjects demonstrated cardiac acceleration, whereas under low-intensity-late-punishment conditions subjects gave evidence of a triphasic cardiac response consisting of two very reliable decelerative components. Such reactions have been used as indices of decreased and increased attention respectively (Graham & Clifton, 1966; Lacey, 1967). Thus, it is suggested that the low-intensity-late-punishment condition facilitated subjects' attention to the verbal remarks immediately following the termination of punishment, whereas the other conditions produced interference of attention to the verbalization of the experimenter.

Subsequent research has tended to confirm such speculation. One study (Cheyne, Goyeche, & Walters, 1969) found that, in the absence of instructions, high-intensity punishment produced cardiac acceleration and greater resistance-to-deviation than low-intensity punishment which resulted in cardiac deceleration. Under conditions in which instructions (behavior rule) were provided, low-intensity punishment was most effective of all (more effective than either high-intensity punishment, whether or not it was followed by instructions, or instructions that were not preceded by punishment). Also supportive of the attentional hypothesis was the finding that subjects under the low-intensity punishment were more likely to look at the experimenter following punishment than subjects under other conditions.

Thus, as the child develops, responses to punishment other than fear or anxiety may take on increasing importance in terms of subsequent resistance-to-deviation. Punishment may be important not so much through its capacity to produce fear or anxiety, but rather as (1) a cue signaling the transgression of a rule, and (2) as a stimulus that may enhance or interfere with attention to accompanying verbalizations. In addition to finding increased resistance-to-deviation under conditions in which training is such as to emphasize the cognitive, informational sources of control as opposed to the affective sources, a number of interesting differences are found:

1. Resistance-to-deviation is *more permanent* over a continuous resistance-to-deviation period (Cheyne, 1971; Cheyne & Walters, 1969; Parke, 1969).

2. There is *greater discrimination* between prohibited and nonprohibited responses (Cheyne 1971).

3. There is greater *denial* of deviation when it occurs (Cheyne & Walters, 1969).

4. There is *less emotional responsivity* (according both to physiological and behavioral indices), during and after punishment, during deviation, and during denial of deviation (Cheyne & Walters, 1970).

The absence of evidence of emotionality under such conditions causes us to suspect that, under certain conditions, the role of anxiety in mediating self-control may become very attenuated. Probably for many instances of self-control in everyday life the rules may, in the absence of anxiety, directly guide behavior as cues that signal certain kinds of responses.

In any case, whatever the role of anxiety, an important role of punishment in older children may be the enhancement of the *explicitness* of the rule in the appropriate situation. Moral philosophers (e.g., R. S. Peters) have suggested that there is a difference between action from habit, and action from reason, there is a difference between being taught "to act in *accordance with* a rule" and "learning to act *on* a rule."

CONCLUSIONS

1. Timing and intensity, in the absence of instructions, have parallel effects to those observed in studies of lower animals.

2. Instructions may modify the effects of variations in the parameters of timing and intensity of punishment.

3. In turn, the specific nature of punishment may influence the state of the organism rendering the instructions either more or less effective.

4. The specific content of instructions (reasoning) may, independently of affective reactions, be instrumental in producing self-control.

5. The informational component of the punishment-reasoning episode may become increasingly important as the child develops.

REFERENCES

Andres, D. H. Modification of delay-of-punishment effects through cognitive restructuring. Unpublished Doctoral thesis, Univ. of Waterloo, 1967.

Aronfreed, J. *Conduct and conscience: the socialization of internalized control over behavior.* New York: Academic Press, 1968.

Aronfreed, J. Punishment control of children's behavior; conditioning, cognition and internalization. Paper presented at the Annual Meeting of the American Psychological Association, New York, 1966.

Aronfreed, J. Punishment learning and internalization: some parameters of reinforcement and cognition. Paper read at Biennial meeting of the Society for Research in Child Development, Minneapolis, March 1965.

Burton, R. V. The generality of morality reconsidered. *Psychological Review,* 1963, 70, 481-499.

Cheyne, J. A. Behavioral and physiological reactions to punishment: attention, anxiety and the timing of punishment hypothesis. Paper presented at the Biennial meeting of the Society for Research in Child Development, 1969.

Cheyne, J. A. Some parameters of punishment affecting resistance to deviation and generalization of a prohibition. *Child Development,* 1971, 42, 1242-1259.

Cheyne, J. A. & Walters, R. H. Timing of punishment, intensity of punishment and cognition structure in resistance-to-deviation. *Journal of Experimental Child Psychology,* 1969, 7, 231-244.

Cheyne, J.A., & Walters, R. H. Some social origins of self-control: Punishment and prohibition. In T. M. Newcomb (Ed.), *New Directions in Psychology.* New York: Holt, 1970. Pp. 279-366.

Cheyne, J. A., Goyeche, J. R. M., & Walters R. H. Attention, anxiety and rules in resistance-to-deviation in children. *Journal of Experimental Child Psychology,* 1969, **8,** 127-139.

Church R. M., Raymond, G. A., & Beauchamp, R. D. Response suppression as a function of intensity and duration of punishment. *Journal of Comparative and Physiological Psychology,* 1967, **63,** 39-44.

Flavell, J. *The developmental psychology of Jean Piaget.* Princeton, N. J.: Van Nostrand, 1963.

Graham, E. K. & Clifton, R. K. Heart-rate change as a component of the orienting response. *Psychological Bulletin,* 1966, **65,** 305-320.

Kohlberg, L. The development of children's orientations toward moral order: I. Sequence in the development of moral thought. *Vita Humana,* 1963, **6,** 11-33.

Kohlberg, L. Development of moral character and moral ideology. *Review of child development,* Russell Sage Foundation, New York, 1964.

Lacey, J. I. Somatic response patterning and stress: some revisions of activation theory. In M. N. Appley and R. Turnbill (Eds.), *Psychological stress: Issues in research.* New York: Appleton-Century-Crofts, 1967.

Leff, R. Effects of punishment intensity and consistency on the internalization of behavioral suppression in children. *Developmental Psychology,* 1969, **1,** 345-356.

Luria, A. R. The genesis of voluntary movements. In N. O'Connor (Ed.), *Recent Soviet psychology.* New York: Liverwright, 1961. Pp. 278-289.

Mandler, G. The interruption of behavior. In D. Levine (Ed.), *Nebraska symposium on motivation: 1964,* Lincoln, Neb.: Univ. of Nebraska Press, 1964.

Mandler, G., & Watson, D. L. Anxiety and the interruption of behavior. In C. D. Spielberger (Ed.), *Anxiety and behavior.* New York: Academic Press, 1966.

Mowrer, O. H. *Learning theory and behavior.* New York: Wiley, 1960.   (a)

Mowrer, O. H. *Learning theory and the symbolic processes.* New York: Wiley, 1960.   (b)

Parke, R. D. Effectiveness of punishment as an interaction of intensity, timing, agent nurturance, and cognitive structuring. *Child Development,* 1969, **40,** 211-235.

Parke, R. D., & Walters, R. H. Some factors influencing the efficacy of punishment training for inducing response inhibition, *Society for Research in Child Development Monographs,* 1967, **32,** No. 1 (Whole No. 109).

Piaget, J. *The moral judgement of the child.* Harcourt, 1932.

Sears, R. R., Maccoby E. E., & Levin H. *Patterns of child rearing.* Evanston, Ill.: Row, Peterson, 1957.

Solomon, R. L., Turner, L. R., & Lessac, M. S. Some effects of delay of punishment on resistance to temptation in dogs. *Journal of Personality and Social Psychology,* 1968, **8,** 233-238.

Walters, R. H., & Parke, R. D., The influence of punishment and related disciplinary techniques on the social behavior of children: Theory and empirical findings. In B. S. Maher (Ed.), *Progress in experimental personality research.* Vol. 3. New York: Academic Press, 1968.

chapter 6

A Developmental Memoir of "Social Learning Theory" | *Justin Aronfreed*

INTRODUCTION

Not very long ago, I had the pleasure of having Dick Walters as an overnight guest at my home. At dinner time, my three children were held spellbound by his description of the conditions of life in the poor Welsh valley community in which he was reared—particularly by the way in which he characterized the very special qualities which were required of a person who wanted to find his way out of the valley.

When the children had retired from the scene, I expressed to Dick, with my tongue well into my cheek, my surprise that a person who conveyed the perspective on socialization that he did in his writing had not placed more emphasis on the point that an individual, no matter how humble his origins, can be molded into something else by education, by the opportunities which are provided in a favorable environment for learning. He replied that he had, in fact, for many years seen himself as an

93

example of how the common clay could be transformed into something else, provided that one felt dedicated to the learning of new skills, and to absorbing the best from one's environment—because it seemed somehow important to him to think that a man could shape his own destiny by exercising control over his experience, no matter what his endowment might have been. Then he added that he had come to feel, in more recent years, that it was no longer so important to him to suppose that anybody could be made into anything, or that people were the product of what they had been determined to absorb from an externally programmed environment. He said that it now seemed to him to detract in no way from his own estimate of his achievements, and that it actually made him feel more at ease with his self-esteem, to think that something intrinsic to himself had, in the last analysis, brought him out of the valley—something in the unfolding of his own capacities which he had imposed upon his environment.

I remember thinking at the time that this change in his view of himself was entirely in accord with other changes which had begun to take place in his view of how to think about children and about what experience could do for them. In the last few years before his untimely death, these changes were reflected in his analysis of the role of distance receptors in the formation of social attachments in human infants, and also in his increasing efforts to characterize the phenomena of observational learning as something more than a problem in the control of children's behavior. He had begun to see these phenomena as an approach to a construction of the child's cognitive and motivational dispositions.

Dick Walters was in a state of transition. He was becoming more intellectually receptive to the ethology of children, to their changing capacities for the representation of reality, and to the structural impositions which they placed on their experience and learning. He was gradually moving away from the conceptual reference points of his earlier interests in the behavior of children, where the central aim was to characterize the child as the product of acquisitions which had moved from the outside to the inside, as a collection of the residues of external inputs, with an allowance for something called "mediating responses" (in recognition of the fact that immediate control by the external environment itself hardly made the child look like a bundle of reflexes). In short, Dick Walters had begun to assume the outlines of a *developmental* psychologist.

Dick would have had many kind words for each of the papers which the other participants have presented. It happens—not by accident, I'm sure—that each one is singularly appropriate to the particular history of the intellectual relationship between Dick and its author. The types of paradigms for analysis of the child's behavior which are espoused in each paper were the types with which he felt at ease. He understood very well their emphasis on description, control, and prediction of behavior. And he could have gone on to contemplate fondly the finer differences between their visions and his own. At the same time, because he was in a state of transition, I think it quite possible that he would have found some larger differences of perspective. What I would like to try to do is to reconstruct briefly some of the things which might have been said from a vantage point that represents the destination of the kind of transition that Dick was going through (even though I don't really know that he would have reached that destination). This is a difficult task for two reasons. To begin with, I cannot recreate his vigor and lust for intellectual combat. My own skills at polemic are very modest. But every one of the other participants in this symposium has known the excitement of a skirmish with Dick in some corner of the forest of the social learning enterprise. Second, it is very difficult to make an estimate of what Dick's intellectual posture would be at precisely this point in time. And so I must finally ask you to recognize that my remarks are my own.

The other participants in this symposium have made my task much easier than I thought it would be, because they too are showing signs of transition—in differing degrees, to be sure, and perhaps subtly enough that the transitions are more visible to me than they are to them. Nevertheless, I think that I detect some signs of progress. And I would like everything that I say here to be construed as encouragement of these transitions. I think that they should be reinforced, because they may lead some day to other and even more interesting transitions. I want to call your attention to the nature of these transitions, to suggest where they might take us if they are allowed to follow their natural course, and to offer a few gentle admonitions not to be frightened by behavioristic ghosts which may lurk in the darkness along the way.

EXPERIMENTS ON PUNISHMENT LEARNING

Dr. Cheyne's experiments on punishment learning and the internalization of behavioral suppression are a significant advance on a line of work that Dick Walters took very seriously, and about which he and I had many long conversations. Perhaps the order and relative emphasis of the inferences which Dr. Cheyne draws are overly modest. They place a great deal of stress on the effects which punishment may have on the child's cognitive representation of the words that are used to structure the punishment situation for him. And they seem to me to glide too quickly over the clear confirmation that his findings provide for a more fundamental point that has emerged from a number of other lines of investigation: that the child's capacity for representation profoundly changes the effectiveness of the punishment itself. The child's cognitive equipment can introduce a radical expansion of the pathways through which the affective consequences of punishment come to exert internalized control over his behavior. This effect is shown in the increased strength of internalized suppression that is produced when children receive verbal communication about their punished behavior. It also appears in the results of the clever techniques which Dr. Cheyne has devised to recreate motoric, iconic, and symbolic representations of transgression at quite long intervals after the child has transgressed.

The question of how punishment may either facilitate or interfere with the child's representational coding of the learning situation, and of what to make of such effects, seems to me to be answered much less clearly. Because I remain uncertain about some of the details of procedure, I do not know quite how to interpret the finding that immediate punishment is *less* effective than delayed punishment under certain conditions in which verbal instructions are given to the child. For example, the instructions were described at one point as being concomitant with immediate punishment, but as another point as having followed the delayed punishment. There is evidence in other work which indicates that the temporal relationship between punishment and verbal explanation has a strong effect on the internalization of behavioral suppression, quite aside from the effect of the immediacy with which the punishment itself follows the occurrence of the transgression. And obviously the interpretation of Dr. Cheyne's findings may be complicated by the use of a loud buzzer to administer the punishment. Such a stimulus might well disturb the child's comprehension of simultaneous verbalization from the adult agent.

Despite the ambiguity in the description of procedure, I think it perfectly valid for Dr. Cheyne to make the point that punishment may affect the cognitive coding process itself—sometimes through its cue or orienting properties, and at other times through its distracting or disruptive affective value. I am not at all persuaded, however, that evidence of stronger internalized suppression and of less "emotionality," when punishment is used at a point where it is presumed not to interfere with the child's representation of the agent's verbal structuring, has any bearing whatsoever on the general utility of a concept of anxiety in making sense of a large body of findings that is now available on children's punishment learning. There might well be less anxiety merely on the basis of the child's better understanding of how to avoid the transgression. But the conceptual function that can be attributed to anxiety, in an account of the child's internalization of behavioral suppression, does not assume that intense emotion is required in order to maintain the internalized control (or even to acquire it). Indices of the activity of the peripheral autonomic nervous system will therefore not be critical in the determination of the value of such a conception. Our problem is to find a consistent set of mechanisms with which we can understand a great variety of results, including the effects of variations in timing and intensity of punishment when the child is not given explicit verbal support for his cognitive capacities. It is difficult to imagine that these mechanisms could, under any conditions, escape the requirement of affective control over the child's overt behavioral commitments—that is, to imagine that conceptions of rules (or of anything else) could exercise an immediate cognitive control over action without the intercession of affective values. One can ascertain simply by talking with children, and by observing their behavior, that they know all kinds of rules which do not necessarily govern their actions.

When one has made the basic transition of recognition that the child's acquisitions from punishment learning can be used to reconstruct his representational capacities, and not only his sensitivity to conditioning parameters, then other interesting paths can be followed. Dr. Cheyne's work already illustrates one such path in the finding that there are age differences in the types of verbal structuring to which children are sensitive in the punishment learning situation. But once we liberalize in this way our ideas about the locus of interesting phenomena in children, we must also make some provision for a careful analysis of the different forms of representation which come to lie within their capacities. Moreover, we need to give more attention to the transformations which children become capable of working in the process of representation. It is not just a question of devising experimental manipulations in the instructions from an adult agent of socialization.

Dr. Cheyne makes a distinction, for example, between the informational specification of a transgression and the more complex verbalization of what he describes as moral or ethical rules. When I looked at some of the appended material at the back of his paper, I discovered that the first level of information actually takes the form: "Do not touch (or play with) that object"—a statement that hardly seems to specify the nature of the transgression much more than does the sheer experience of punishment. If such a statement produces a gain in the effectiveness of the child's internalized behavioral suppression, it may do so because of what it adds to the explicitness or intensity of prohibition, rather than because of what it adds to the child's cognitive resources for a mobile representation of the category of transgressions. Likewise, the statement: "That belongs to someone else" is given as an example of a moral rule (along with a characterization of such statements as falling into the form: "X is a member of a particular class"). This last example would give the child a more abstract representation of the forbidden class of actions. But the verbalization of a class attribute of belongingness or possession will not necessarily establish the kinds of representational operators which might properly be described as rules. Nor will it provide the evaluative dimensions which would meet any interesting criteria for a *moral* concept. It is important to make such distinctions, because they may point us toward the underlying processes and structures which make it meaningful to study age differences in the first place.

RESPONSE-LEARNING THEORY

Dr. Gewirtz's paper casts a spell on me. I knew that it would. It is an excellent presentation of the program or metatheory that he has applied to a wide range of phenomena. And the intended scope of this program speaks for itself. It is the scope that accounts for the fact that Dr. Gewirtz was always encountering Dick Walters somewhere in the forest. There were very few scientific interests which they did not share, and even fewer on which they could agree. As an innocent bystander, I continue to admire the systematic ambitions of Dr. Gewirtz's program. It may represent a glorious last stand for radical behaviorism. But it is a very thoughtful and analytic behaviorism—not a casual one—and it expands to the outer limits the viability of the kind of thinking that can be called, with some oversimplification, "response-learning theory." Behind the behavior of the child lies the stimulus inputs and outcomes of an external environment, together with whatever stable dispositions the environment may have already induced. And I have always been an awed observer of the epistemological pyrotechnics which can be brought to the defense and elaboration of this conception of the child.

But after all of the contextual determinants and their relationships to specific stimulus values have been taken into account, I have still not been able to understand how their impact on the child can be characterized without reference to the structure that the child imposes on them. The deficiency in my understanding cannot possibly be attributed to Dr. Gewirtz's exposition, the message of which is unmistakably clear. And it certainly cannot be my fault. I have been forced to consider the possibility that there may be something missing in the program. I thought that I detected in Dr. Gewirtz's remarks some evidence of a cautious exploration of the same possibility. Since it is apparent that stimulus values and reinforcing events are not sufficiently predictive to handle an organism so perverse as a child, he suggests that we turn our attention to the contextual or setting conditions which qualify control of the child's behavior. It turns out that these conditions are quite formidable. They are complex and difficult to formulate as observable descriptions of the external environment. One then begins to wonder whether the contextual determinants will ever be comprehensible unless they are conceptualized with reference to a theoretical construction of the child—a construction that specifies some of the cognitive impositions which the child will place on his surroundings.

The allowance for contextual determinants already grants the problem that specific external stimulus values are not a powerfully reliable medium of control over the child's behavior. We should therefore be willing to dare to ask whether the behavior may not be more usefully thought of as being controlled by the child—in which case we are both fortunate and informed when we can find some forms of external stimulus display or information which do appear to enter into the behavioral control. We might then use such observations to construct a model of the child's intrinsic psychological structure.

Of course, the penalty for asking such questions is that we may have to tolerate what Dr. Gewirtz calls "excess meanings" (or what are known in other contexts as theoretical ideas). But I note that certain kinds of excess meanings emerge, at various points in his paper, as interesting ways of talking about the child's behavior. For example, he gives some importance to another person's social role as a contextual source of control over the child's behavior. But no mention is made of the fact that the child must have a conception of the relevant role in order for the role to act as a determinant of his actions. Dr. Gewirtz's children are not permitted to have states of "arousal" or "anxiety" (these words appear in quotation marks in his paper). But they do have states of deprivation and satiation. They also have levels of aspiration and preferences for one sex of an experimental agent over another. For the time being, we can take some satisfaction in these allowances. But I would be less than honest if I did not admit that I cherish, in the back of my mind, the hope that his children will also eventually prove to have minds.

GENERALIZED IMITATION

I hardly know where to begin the many reinforcements which I want to dispense to the ideas which Dr. Hartup has expressed. His paper is another example of the kinds of conceptual redefinitions that Dick Walters was beginning to experience in his own thinking about the problem of imitation. It makes many points which are well worth our attention for some time to come. I share Dr. Hartup's perception that the concept of generalized imitation has been used in ways which tend to obscure the importance of more reflective conceptual analyses and distinctions among different classes of phenomena. But I am less sanguine than he is about the prospect of getting a better theory through further parametric experimental work on stimulus and response dimensions, gradients, or reinforcement schedules. Likewise, I doubt that we will learn very much simply from correlations which attempt to establish changes with increasing age in the degree of generalization that children's imitation shows across different tasks.

As Dr. Hartup points out, reinforcement history and contiguity notions of learning are rather inadequate as explanations of the basic phenomenon in imitation—the one that permits the child to generate so quickly an imitative behavioral product in the first place. However, I am less certain that infancy should be singled out as the most vulnerable point in a social learning perspective. The concepts of learning which come from that perspective seem to me to be no more persuasive an account of the many phenomena which collectively have been called "imitation" in the case of older children, even though it may be true that it is easier to obtain an appearance of generalized process in older children. That appearance may be attributable to the fact that the cognitive resources of older children have greater equilibrium or breadth of applicability to different situations.

The transitions which Dr. Hartup wants to make spring from his perception that the analysis of what is called "imitation," in the social learning tradition, assumes certain generalized and functional relationships between the behavior that the child observes and the consequences in his own behavior. It is not an analysis that is geared to the developmental status of the child. He suggests that we give more attention to changes of the imitative repertoire over time, as the child's capacities emerge, as well as to situational variation in the repertoire. I hope and expect that he would carry this approach beyond assessments of children's behavior at different ages, and under different conditions, to a consideration of the strategies for construction of the underlying mechanisms which differentiate the various classes of phenomena that can be uncovered. Developmental analysis cannot be carried very far if we have merely a catalogue of the different kinds of behavior which are imitated as the child grows older. Nor is it sufficient to record that the behavioral effects of the child's opportunity to observe others become increasingly independent of the immediate presence of a model. What is required also is some conceptually informed classification of the variety of phenomena which are often indiscriminately collected under labels such as "imitation" or "observational learning." Then there must be an attempt to infer from the different classes, and from their relationships to age and to one another, the mechanisms that reveal the nature and order of the consecutive psychological constitutions which children may acquire over the course of changes in their experience and capacity. It is from such analyses that one would begin to perceive the sequential and hierarchical relationships which are the essence of a developmental analysis.

The idea that developmental psychologists should be especially concerned with maintenance and transfer of imitation seems to me to underestimate the magnitude of the problem, which is one of characterizing the very nature of imitative acquisitions in the first place. In fact, it is easy to imagine that certain kinds of developmental advances may be indexed in the *lack* of maintenance or transfer of an imitative repertoire. Age or time variables in themselves will add little to the kind of analysis of imitation that focusses primarily on external stimulus controls. Very careful attention must also be given to changes in the child's cognitive resources, which construct the child's commerce with his environment even as they continue to build upon it.

Part of what needs attention here can perhaps be illustrated in Dr. Hartup's use of terms such as "mediational activity" and "representational behavior" when he is speaking of the verbalization that the child either produces or receives. But if we are talking about the child's overtly observable actions, or about the stimulus events to which the child is being exposed, then the description of these actions or events might not in itself require a concept of representation. The concept of representation is required because we want to account for the fact that verbalization does exercise some control over the child's behavior—because it is necessary to assign existence and some properties to a symbolic medium. Dr. Hartup reports the interesting finding that there are age differences in the amount of benefit that a child's observational learning will derive from different conditions of verbalization. It is at least equally interesting to raise the following question: How shall we reconstruct the order in which different capacities or structures come into being in a remarkable organism which, at a certain point in its development, will not spontaneously use verbal coding of a model's behavior, but which can benefit when the verbal code is imposed from without? The question is interesting because it carries implications for the different types of relationship which may exist between the child's capacity for language and his capacity for a variety of other forms of cognitive representation.

Early imitative actions may differ from later imitation not only in terms of surface features, such as the particular act matched, the role of attention, and the amount of prestructuring or tuning that is externally given to the child's behavior (as in the device of putting the child through the required movements), but also in terms of the very nature of the relationship between the child's behavior and the model's behavior, the form of which may be imposed by what are at first the child's very limited representational capacities. None of these considerations should be used, in my opinion, to pose an artificial discrepancy between developmental concepts and the pursuit of imitation as a form of learning. There is no inconsistency between developmental phenomena and the assumption that imitation can be treated as a very powerful form of learning. Inconsistency arises only when learning is conceptualized merely as a process in which internal residues are left from external engagements, and in which any specificity of control over the child's behavior must be attributed to the inherent properties of external events.

THEORIES OF MODELLING

Dr. Bandura's paper is a review of his work on the phenomena which he has treated as evidence of children's learning through a process of modelling. Their mutual interest in the behavioral effects of children's opportunities for social observation was an important component of the attraction that drew Dr. Bandura and Richard Walters together for a number of years of fruitful collaboration. Since I am primarily interested in indices of conceptual transition, I will not dwell on Dr. Bandura's critique of a Skinnerian analysis of imitation. He has made it effectively on earlier occasions. And it is clearly appropriate to his recognition that a representation of the model is required for imitative learning. Analyses of imitation in terms of operant discrimination training do not concern themselves with the child's capacity for representation, because they address themselves only to the external events which appear to exercise control over the child's behavioral performance.

I am in agreement with some of the issues which Dr. Bandura poses as problems for a satisfactory account of imitation. For example, it is clear that there is a problem in specifying the source of reinforcement—essentially a problem in the affective control of the child's behavioral product. There is also a problem in the fact that the child's imitation may be successfully delayed well beyond the point of original exposure to a model. However, this last problem in itself may not be too important in deciding between alternative theoretical conceptions. I would point to a more critical problem which has not received sufficient attention. The problem is that the child's imitation must meet demanding criteria of sequence, structure, and behavioral topography even before potential external sources of reinforcement can be brought into play. Because of the speed and fidelity with which imitative learning can occur, it seems obvious that this latter problem cannot be resolved merely by appeals to the power of reinforcement schedules, or to the pervasiveness of response drift and generalization.

Dr. Bandura's current perspective raises two other issues which seem to me to come quite close to the heart of the problem of imitation. He suggests first that the behavior which children show in many of his paradigms of observational learning represents a form of modelling that is not bound to specific stimulus situations. It is asserted that the children in these paradigms derive rules or principles from their observation of the behavior of others. The effects which are obtained clearly do offer a parallel to the great transituational mobility of which children's imitative dispositions are capable under naturalistic conditions. But I think that it remains a very open question as to how much independence of concrete external cues could be inferred from a close empirical analysis of the paradigms. Certainly, it would seem that the kinds of behavioral effects of observation which are usually demonstrated could often be accounted for by representational capacities which are substantially less powerful than what is implied in the concept of a rule or a principle.

Secondly, Dr. Bandura notes that the imitative behavior of children often has not only innovative but also generative properties. I think that this observation is a significant advance over what I perceive to have been his earlier emphasis on the merely reflective fidelity of the surface of the child's behavior as a criterion of imitative learning. The mobile, saltatory, innovative, and generative properties of children's imitation all can be combined, for purposes of theoretical confrontation, into one large question: What is the nature of the creature who is capable of such a remarkable form of learning? I thought it a very interesting sign of transition that Dr. Bandura has begun to answer this question with an increasing frequency of reference to representational learning, even though he also continues to speak of the child's acquisition of "responses." We have opened for ourselves, then, the challenging task of trying to determine the forms of representation which are engaged by children's imitation, and of then trying to ascertain the processes through which these representations are acquired. Among the various approaches to the task which Dr. Bandura has suggested, it appears to me that some are more likely to be illuminating than others.

1. It does not seem that a focus on attentional processes promises in itself to be very revealing. Attention is clearly a prerequisite of any form of observational learning, regardless of what kinds of representational (or even nonrepresentational) capacities are specified in an acquisition theory. If the child does not attend at some level, he is not likely to learn anything by observation.

2. Likewise, the child's capacity for retention or storage must always be assumed as a prerequisite for observational learning, and would not seem to be critical in distinguishing among different viable conceptions of the learning process. We would do better to ask about the *form* in which the observed behavior of a model is stored, because this question takes us back to the more primary one concerning the very nature of the representation.

3. The notion of rehearsal also does not add very much to a conception of the acquisition problem in imitation. Whether the rehearsal is assumed to be overt or covert, its very existence presumes that something to be rehearsed already has been acquired (although this acquisition may be consolidated, of course, by the rehearsal).

4. When we get into the area of what Dr. Bandura now calls "coding operations," we are coming much closer to the central problem of the child's capacity for representational acquisitions. However, it seems to me a damaging oversimplification to suppose that these acquisitions all can be embraced under the label of symbolic processes. Symbolic representation is very high powered. And there are many reasons to think, on the basis of common observation alone, that children's imitative acquisitions do not necessarily require storage in symbolic form. Dr. Bandura's own demonstrations of imitation, and of other kinds of observational control of behavior, frequently give evidence of strong representational capacities in young children. Yet many of the behavioral effects which are obtained give no explicit indication that the representational medium is truly symbolic.

Of course, there is a problem of definition here. Dr. Bandura apparently is using the term *symbolic* to include both his categories of imaginal (iconic) and verbal (linguistic) representation. This usage is a very broad one. It does not allow for the interesting distinctions which can be made among different forms of representation when the term *symbolic* is restricted to representational media which have certain special assets and constraints (among which is the formidable advantage of an arbitrary assignment of relationship between symbol and an external sample of referent events). The imitative behavior of children, and of young children in particular, may often be dependent on imagery which is more like an iconic and motoric copy than it is like anything that can be said to have the properties of a symbol. The child may also have a number of powerful operators or transformations which can be used directly on iconic representations to give imitation its great mobility or freedom from concrete external stimulus situations. Moreover, the imitative learning of children may well engage other forms of representation which are more abstract and hierarchical than iconic imagery, but which do not use the symbolic medium of language.

I am surprised to find the implicit assumption that representation based on *perceptual* inputs should be able to monitor the complex sequence and motor topography of the imitative performances of which children are capable. From the child's point of view, representation based only on direct perception of samples of observed behavior would be extremely limited as a template for the child's reproduction of the behavior. For example, children are dependent on the visual modality for much of their observation of the nonverbal behavior of potential models. But their reproduction of the behavior would not ordinarily produce anything like the visual form of the information that was coded from the original model, since the extent to which they can "see" their motor reproduction is quite negligible. The discrepancy between the original mode of input and the available perceptual feedback from an imitative performance presents no problem, however, if the performance is under the control of a cognitive template that represents an imposed transformation and organization of the original input. Control of the match in the imitative behavior would then be mobile—that is, free of the requirement of a self-produced fidelity to a concrete visual representation of the model.

Control of the fidelity of the match is a more general problem for any theoretical account of imitative learning. But it is an especially awkward problem for an account that rests on a concept of sensory conditioning through contiguity. If the child's own imitative performance can be independent of the cues which are provided in the presence of the model, as is obviously the case, then it is necessary to look elsewhere for the stimulus side of a contiguity bond—the side that would later activate the child's representation of the model even in the model's absence. It is no solution to suppose that the child's representations can be treated as "perceptual responses" which become attached to situational cues or other stimulus events. For we are then still confronted with the problem of how the child is able to control the behavioral flow of an imitative performance with great precision when the self-produced feedback could not possibly match a direct perceptual representation of the model. And more generally, mere contiguity between any two kinds of inputs does not begin to specify the source of the sequential and structural properties of children's imitative capacities.

That verbalization may facilitate the observational learning process is both interesting and important. But it is only one ingredient for a broader conceptualization of representational control over imitative behavior. Verbal facilitation raises the more fundamental question of what language contributes specifically to the child's representation of a model's behavior, so that the stored representation can more readily be unfolded into an accurate imitative performance. It also points to the problem of comparison among different forms of representation in the extent of their power to reproduce different kinds of behavioral fidelity to a model (for example, fidelity of the sensory-motor surface topography of behavior as opposed to a deeper structural fidelity in the relationships among components of the behavior).

Dr. Bandura also notes the importance of incentives and motivational processes in the control of overt imitative performance. Affective control of a child's imitative behavioral performance is a relatively neglected aspect of the requirements of a theory of imitation. It would be useful to attempt to specify, for example, how affectivity becomes coupled to a child's cognitive representation of a model. Since imitative behavior presumably must be governed by potential affective values even before it attains overt performance, the affective values cannot be divorced from the representations which control the form of the imitative behavior. The affective value of various components of the original model's behavior may also determine which components receive attention and storage in the first place. Dr. Bandura showed some awareness of this latter point in his application of a concept of selective discrimination to phenomena which are sometimes regarded as evidence of "generalized imitation." A discriminative monitor in the child's imitation would certainly need to be under the control of affective value.

There is one final point that I wish to make, because it seems to me to capture much of the perspective of these comments on the problems of a theory of imitation. In a paper that appeared recently in the *Psychological Review,* Gewirtz and Stingle questioned the value of theories of imitation which invoke representational processes, in part on the grounds that these processes can only be inferred and are not directly observable. As it happens, Dr. Bandura's transgressions in this respect are relatively minor compared to my own. Yet in his paper for this symposium, he felt called upon to explain that the sin of inferring representation in the child's mind applies only to theories which attribute behavior to "hypothetical internal agencies," and that symbolic events are independently manipulated rather than only inferred in his experiments. As I understand his defense, he and Dr. Gewirtz are in agreement on the purity of not drawing any inferences about representation from the child's behavior. But it seems to me only that they are more comfortable with invisible external agencies than with hypothetical internal agencies. Actually, in the experiments to which Dr. Bandura refers, it is verbalization or speech, and not symbolic representation, that is being subjected to controlled experimental manipulation. And the interesting results which are obtained may quite properly be used to infer the presence of symbolic representation. There is always the possibility of being able to infer correctly, and thus of reaping the reward of an understanding of the child's behavior.

REFERENCE

Gewirtz, J. L., & Stingle, K. G. The learning of generalized imitation as a basis for identification. *Psychological Review*, 1968, **75**, 374-397.

Author Index

109

Subject Index

113